Table of Contents - Level 3B

this new 3B booklet we learn A TON! We will learn the correct LONG multiplication and LONG vision. Do not worry: it does not take long at all to figure them out. We will get our first taste of OWERS a few years ahead of grade level, but thats OK: they really are a child's play and very easy to derstand.

e will look at some OPTICAL ILLUSIONS and see what we e is not always what we think it is. We'll continue to explore eometry through studying 2 dimensional shapes and 3 mensional solids. We will keep playing our games, INKYs, usokus, 3-Dice, 4-Dice, and SO MUCH MORE

NJOY THE JOURNEY! From us all at Renert's Bright Minds and Renert School

Renert's Bright Minds expresses its gratitude to Jack Hope, Barbara and Bob Reys for creating this wonderful resource and allowing our students to use it throughout the program.

Mental Math
in the Middle Grades
Jack A. Hope   Barbara J. Reys   Robert E. Reys

LESSON 10   STARTING AT THE LEFT

When you add with pencil and paper, you usually start at the **right** and work toward the left.

To add in your head, try starting at the **left.**

THINK . . .

48 + 27

40 plus 20 is 60,

and 8 plus 7 is 15 . . .

60 plus 15 is 75.

Try this one from the left.

55 + 28

50 + 20 is 70 . . .

5 + 8 is 13 . . .

70 + 13 is 83.

TRY THESE IN YOUR HEAD.

Start at the left and add.

1. 35 + 49   3. 26 + 47   7. 55 + 29
2. 53 + 28   4. 19 + 37   8. 44 + 27
                   5. 15 + 65   9. 19 + 63
                   6. 47 + 28   10. 36 + 49

POWER BUILDER A

1. 28 + 15 = _____
2. 47 + 25 = _____
3. 18 + 24 = _____
4. 65 + 25 = _____
5. 53 + 19 = _____
6. 45 + 27 = _____
7. 38 + 24 = _____
8. 43 + 38 = _____
9. 15 + 65 = _____
10. 29 + 45 = _____

11. 54 + 28 = _____
12. 25 + 18 = _____
13. 36 + 45 = _____
14. 19 + 65 = _____
15. 57 + 26 = _____
16. 17 + 35 = _____
17. 79 + 18 = _____
18. 54 + 29 = _____
19. 45 + 36 = _____
20. 28 + 27 = _____

THINK IT THROUGH

If this is not a leap year, what is the date of the 100th day of the year?

MENTAL MATH IN THE MIDDLE GRADES   LESSON 10   STARTING AT THE LEFT

POWER BUILDER B

1. 24 + 19 = _____
2. 68 + 24 = _____
3. 19 + 18 = _____
4. 34 + 47 = _____
5. 65 + 15 = _____
6. 29 + 15 = _____
7. 17 + 25 = _____
8. 19 + 37 = _____
9. 48 + 15 = _____
10. 26 + 55 = _____

11. 35 + 18 = _____
12. 17 + 49 = _____
13. 45 + 47 = _____
14. 37 + 28 = _____
15. 16 + 35 = _____
16. 69 + 18 = _____
17. 15 + 49 = _____
18. 23 + 28 = _____
19. 35 + 47 = _____
20. 26 + 39 = _____

THINK IT THROUGH

If you think of January 1 as day 1 and December 31 as day 365 (it is not a leap year), what day is May 28?

2

LESSON 11   STARTING AT THE LEFT

Subtraction problems come in two styles . . .

THOSE THAT **NEED** REGROUPING	436 – 28 5227 – 2981

THOSE THAT **DON'T NEED** REGROUPING	436 – 23 5227 – 2125

When they don't need regrouping,
you can start at either end.

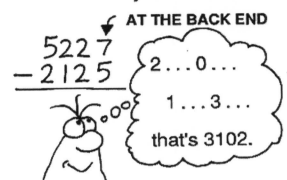

AT THE BACK END

$$5227$$
$$-2125$$

2 . . . 0 . . .

1 . . . 3 . . .

that's 3102.

AT THE FRONT END

$$5227$$
$$-2125$$

3 . . . 1 . . .

0 . . . 2 . . .

3102.

Starting at the front end makes
more sense because then you
don't have to juggle digits.

TRY THESE IN YOUR HEAD.

Start at the front end and subtract.

1. 47 – 26	**3.** 49 – 18	**7.** 5647 – 3515
2. 84 – 61	**4.** 357 – 135	**8.** 6892 – 1812
	5. 846 – 715	**9.** 7368 – 4317
	6. 947 – 645	**10.** 4807 – 1503

POWER BUILDER A

1. 99 − 35 = _____
2. 49 − 17 = _____
3. 58 − 24 = _____
4. 45 − 20 = _____
5. 67 − 33 = _____
6. 85 − 71 = _____
7. 156 − 50 = _____
8. 348 − 25 = _____
9. 265 − 54 = _____
10. 893 − 82 = _____

11. 475 − 150 = _____
12. 289 − 125 = _____
13. 850 − 130 = _____
14. 777 − 234 = _____
15. 594 − 203 = _____
16. 6517 − 2500 = _____
17. 8765 − 1234 = _____
18. 5029 − 4020 = _____
19. 6894 − 333 = _____
20. 9876 − 540 = _____

THINK IT THROUGH

The difference between two numbers is 10. If the numbers are doubled, what is the difference between them?

MENTAL MATH IN THE MIDDLE GRADES

LESSON 11   STARTING AT THE LEFT

POWER BUILDER B

1. 99 − 54 = _____
2. 57 − 14 = _____
3. 37 − 23 = _____
4. 64 − 30 = _____
5. 47 − 22 = _____
6. 75 − 24 = _____
7. 185 − 40 = _____
8. 275 − 25 = _____
9. 486 − 75 = _____
10. 575 − 64 = _____

11. 365 − 125 = _____
12. 780 − 250 = _____
13. 984 − 430 = _____
14. 888 − 345 = _____
15. 687 − 505 = _____
16. 3527 − 1300 = _____
17. 6895 − 5050 = _____
18. 7533 − 1301 = _____
19. 7856 − 250 = _____
20. 9999 − 444 = _____

THINK IT THROUGH

The difference between two numbers is 25. If the numbers are doubled, what is the difference between them?

54

LESSON 19 THINK QUARTERS

Does counting by 25 seem hard to you?

Try thinking of quarters.

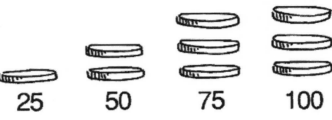

25   50   75   100

Think of counting out $5 in quarters.

25	50	75	100
125	150	175	200
225	250	275	300
325	350	375	400
425	450	475	500

What pattern do you see?

Use that pattern to help you add these in your head.

125 + 25 + 25 = ?

75 + 25 + 50 = ?

TRY THESE IN YOUR HEAD.

Think quarters.

1. 50 + 25
2. 150 + 25
3. 250 + 25
4. 225 + 25 + 25
5. 100 + 25 + 25

6. 350 + 25
7. 75 + 50
8. 225 + 50
9. 250 + 75 + 25
10. 125 + 25 + 50 + 25

POWER BUILDER A

1. 75 + 25 = _____
2. 50 + 25 = _____
3. 225 + 25 = _____
4. 100 + 25 + 25 = _____
5. 300 + 50 = _____
6. 175 + 25 + 25 = _____
7. 75 + 50 = _____
8. 75 + 25 + 50 = _____
9. 325 + 50 = _____
10. 225 + 25 + 50 = _____

11. 175 + 25 + 25 = _____
12. 650 + 25 + 50 = _____
13. 400 + 75 + 50 = _____
14. 50 + 75 + 25 = _____
15. 250 + 75 + 50 = _____
16. 350 + 75 + 50 = _____
17. 425 + 50 + 75 = _____
18. 200 + 75 + 50 = _____
19. 325 + 50 + 75 = _____
20. 250 + 75 + 75 = _____

THINK IT THROUGH

Suppose you had five quarters. Then someone gave you twice as many more. How much money do you have now?

POWER BUILDER B

1. 150 + 25 = _____
2. 75 + 25 = _____
3. 325 + 25 = _____
4. 200 + 50 + 25 = _____
5. 400 + 50 = _____
6. 275 + 25 + 25 = _____
7. 175 + 50 = _____
8. 75 + 25 + 50 = _____
9. 425 + 50 = _____
10. 325 + 25 + 50 = _____

11. 275 + 50 = _____
12. 550 + 25 + 50 = _____
13. 200 + 75 + 50 = _____
14. 150 + 75 + 25 = _____
15. 250 + 75 + 50 = _____
16. 550 + 75 + 50 = _____
17. 825 + 50 + 75 = _____
18. 300 + 50 + 75 = _____
19. 625 + 50 + 75 = _____
20. 350 + 75 + 75 = _____

THINK IT THROUGH

Suppose you had ten quarters. Then someone gave you half as much as you already had. But then you lost one quarter. How much money do you have now?

4

LESSON 20   NOTICING NINES

Did you ever wonder
why so many prices
end in 98 and 99?

Studies show that more
people will buy something
priced at $9.99 than at $10.
That's why we see prices like these.

In mental math, you can clean up numbers
ending in 8 or 9 to make them easy to add.

Round up . . .   add . . .   then adjust.

$$300 + 450 \rightarrow 750$$
$$\underline{-1}$$
$$749$$

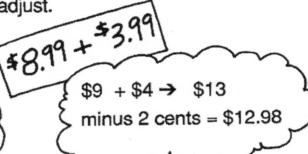

$$\$9 + \$4 \rightarrow \$13$$

minus 2 cents = $12.98

TRY THESE IN YOUR HEAD.

Clean up the 8's and 9's.

1. 65 + 29	**3.** 254 + 499	**7.** $2.75 + $1.99
2. 88 + 69	**4.** 478 + 899	**8.** $11.50 + $3.99
	5. 265 + 98	**9.** $59.80 + $8.99
	6. 4314 + 898	**10.** $19.98 + $25.50

POWER BUILDER A

1. 35 + 29 = _____
2. 54 + 49 = _____
3. 26 + 98 = _____
4. 45 + 39 = _____
5. 56 + 29 = _____
6. 125 + 99 = _____
7. 423 + 498 = _____
8. 807 + 99 = _____
9. 244 + 699 = _____
10. 1524 + 299 = _____

11. $3.22 + $1.99 = _____
12. $0.75 + $0.98 = _____
13. $2.85 + $1.98 = _____
14. $15.35 + $0.98 = _____
15. $7.45 + $9.98 = _____
16. $4.25 + $1.99 = _____
17. $0.98 + $0.65 = _____
18. $2.35 + $1.99 = _____
19. $13.45 + $10.98 = _____
20. $5.98 + $9.99 = _____

THINK IT THROUGH

The price of a daily paper at the newsstand is $0.35 per copy. The regular subscription rate is $0.24 per copy. How much can you save per week by subscribing rather than buying a paper daily?

MENTAL MATH IN THE MIDDLE GRADES

POWER BUILDER B

1. 25 + 49 = _____
2. 63 + 28 = _____
3. 45 + 98 = _____
4. 154 + 99 = _____
5. 199 + 267 = _____
6. 456 + 399 = _____
7. 2145 + 699 = _____
8. 399 + 198 = _____
9. 4256 + 498 = _____
10. 298 + 275 = _____

11. $0.26 + $0.99 = _____
12. $2.45 + $1.99 = _____
13. $0.87 + $0.98 = _____
14. $1.45 + $0.98 = _____
15. $4.52 + $4.99 = _____
16. $15.99 + $2.65 = _____
17. $7.98 + $9.75 = _____
18. $5.35 + $19.99 = _____
19. $45.86 + $29.99 = _____
20. $7.98 + $18.75 = _____

THINK IT THROUGH

The price of a monthly magazine at the newsstand is $1.75. The subscription rate is $1.00 per issue. How much can you save in a year by subscribing rather than buying the magazine monthly?

76

LESSON 21   NOTICING NINES

To **add** 8's and 9's in your head, you clean them up by rounding to "make tens," then adjust the answer.

$.99 + $1.99

$1 + $2 → $3 minus 2 cents or $2.98

Here's good news: The same idea works for subtraction!

75 − 29

75 − 30 → 45
+ 1

46

827 − 198

827 − 200 → 627
+ 2

629

$20 − $15.98

$20 − $16 → $4 plus 2 cents = $4.02

TRY THESE IN YOUR HEAD.

Clean up the 8's and 9's.

1. 83 − 39
2. 95 − 59
3. 427 − 198
4. 872 − 399
5. 265 − 98
6. 5236 − 999
7. $8.36 − $5.99
8. $20 − $13.98
9. $40 − $29.99
10. $100 − $59.98

POWER BUILDER A

1. 82 − 29 = _____
2. 45 − 19 = _____
3. 265 − 98 = _____
4. 74 − 49 = _____
5. 81 − 28 = _____
6. 436 − 189 = _____
7. 724 − 199 = _____
8. 615 − 98 = _____
9. 246 − 198 = _____
10. 1754 − 999 = _____

11. $5.00 − $1.99 = _____
12. $5.00 − $0.98 = _____
13. $5.00 − $3.99 = _____
14. $10.00 − $3.98 = _____
15. $20.00 − $9.98 = _____
16. $20.00 − $14.99 = _____
17. $5.00 − $2.98 = _____
18. $10.00 − $4.99 = _____
19. $50.00 − $29.99 = _____
20. $20.00 − $4.98 = _____

THINK IT THROUGH

If you buy a pair of jeans for $11.99 and a belt for $5.99, how much change will you get back from $20.00? (Don't figure any tax.)

MENTAL MATH IN THE MIDDLE GRADES   LESSON 21   NOTICING NINES

POWER BUILDER B

1. 64 − 29 = _____
2. 83 − 49 = _____
3. 75 − 48 = _____
4. 246 − 199 = _____
5. 435 − 299 = _____
6. 1527 − 999 = _____
7. 752 − 198 = _____
8. 4526 − 998 = _____
9. 1800 − 499 = _____
10. 1750 − 198 = _____

11. $0.75 − $0.59 = _____
12. $0.50 − $0.28 = _____
13. $2.00 − $0.98 = _____
14. $10.00 − $4.98 = _____
15. $20.00 − $15.99 = _____
16. $100.00 − $49.99 = _____
17. $50.00 − $19.98 = _____
18. $20.00 − $12.98 = _____
19. $20.00 − $8.99 = _____
20. $50.00 − $18.99 = _____

THINK IT THROUGH

If you buy one T-shirt for $8.98 and two records at $4.99 each, how much change will you get back from $20.00? (Don't figure any tax.)

78

LESSON 22   TACK ON TRAILING ZEROS

Here's a simple way to multiply any number by 10, or 100, or 1000, in your head.

Look for a pattern in the zeros.

5 × 10 = 5 **tens** = 50
5 × 100 = 5 **hundreds** = 500
5 × 1000 = 5 **thousands** = 5000

To multiply any number . . .

by 10	→	tack on ONE trailing zero.
by 100	→	tack on TWO trailing zeros.
by 1000	→	tack on THREE trailing zeros.

Here's how
a mental-math
pro thinks . . .

9 **thousands** . . . so tack on three zeros after the 9.
9000

TRY THESE IN YOUR HEAD.
Tack on trailing zeros.

1. 3 × 10	**3.** 8 × 1000	**7.** 100 × 8
2. 7 × 100	**4.** 10 × 13	**8.** 7 × 1000
	5. 23 × 100	**9.** 1000 × 14
	6. 1000 × 11	**10.** 10 × 162

POWER BUILDER A

1. 2 × 10 = _____
2. 5 × 10 = _____
3. 10 × 7 = _____
4. 4 × 100 = _____
5. 3 × 100 = _____
6. 1000 × 5 = _____
7. 7 × 1000 = _____
8. 2 × 1000 = _____
9. 8 × 100 = _____
10. 10 × 9 = _____

11. 11 × 10 = _____
12. 10 × 27 = _____
13. 125 × 10 = _____
14. 23 × 100 = _____
15. 69 × 100 = _____
16. 125 × 100 = _____
17. 13 × 1000 = _____
18. 1000 × 18 = _____
19. 275 × 1000 = _____
20. 1000 × 51 = _____

THINK IT THROUGH

If I pay 26 cents for a paper and sell it for 35 cents, how much money will I make selling 100 papers?

MENTAL MATH IN THE MIDDLE GRADES · LESSON 22 TACK ON TRAILING ZEROS

POWER BUILDER B

1. 4 × 10 = _____
2. 6 × 10 = _____
3. 10 × 3 = _____
4. 2 × 100 = _____
5. 6 × 100 = _____
6. 1000 × 3 = _____
7. 6 × 1000 = _____
8. 4 × 1000 = _____
9. 100 × 7 = _____
10. 15 × 100 = _____

11. 13 × 10 = _____
12. 19 × 10 = _____
13. 10 × 25 = _____
14. 27 × 100 = _____
15. 100 × 73 = _____
16. 375 × 100 = _____
17. 19 × 1000 = _____
18. 375 × 1000 = _____
19. 1000 × 12 = _____
20. 1000 × 68 = _____

THINK IT THROUGH

John bought a baseball card for 30 cents and sold it for 45 cents. He then bought it back for 40 cents and sold it again for 50 cents. How much money did he make?

80

LESSON 23   TACK ON TRAILING ZEROS

Here's a trick for multiplying in your head.
Look at the zeros. What's the pattern?

$5 \times 30 = 5 \times 3$ **tens** $= 15 \times 10 = 150$
$7 \times 400 = 7 \times 4$ **hundreds** $= 28 \times 100 = 2800$
$6 \times 3000 = 6 \times 3$ **thousands** $= 18 \times 1000 = 18,000$

When one number has trailing zeros . . .

    1. Cut off the trailing zeros.

     2. Multiply the remaining numbers.

     3. Tack the trailing zeros onto your answer.

Here's how a mental-math pro thinks . . .

TRY THESE IN YOUR HEAD.
Tack on the right number of zeros.

1. 5×30	**3.** 8×800	**7.** 8×70
2. 60×4	**4.** 9×40	**8.** 7×700
	5. 2×4000	**9.** 200×13
	6. 12×200	**10.** 3000×8

POWER BUILDER A

1. $4 \times 80 =$ _____
2. $70 \times 7 =$ _____
3. $9 \times 90 =$ _____
4. $80 \times 3 =$ _____
5. $12 \times 30 =$ _____
6. $4 \times 500 =$ _____
7. $900 \times 5 =$ _____
8. $800 \times 6 =$ _____
9. $8 \times 300 =$ _____
10. $12 \times 200 =$ _____

11. $3000 \times 9 =$ _____
12. $4 \times 2000 =$ _____
13. $8 \times 3000 =$ _____
14. $7 \times 7000 =$ _____
15. $12 \times 4000 =$ _____
16. $7 \times 6000 =$ _____
17. $8 \times 90 =$ _____
18. $500 \times 5 =$ _____
19. $8 \times 7000 =$ _____
20. $4 \times 400 =$ _____

THINK IT THROUGH

Which are worth more: 40 nickels or 25 dimes?

LESSON 23   TACK ON TRAILING ZEROS

POWER BUILDER B

1. $8 \times 80 =$ _____
2. $10 \times 7 =$ _____
3. $9 \times 30 =$ _____
4. $80 \times 4 =$ _____
5. $12 \times 20 =$ _____
6. $5 \times 500 =$ _____
7. $900 \times 2 =$ _____
8. $800 \times 2 =$ _____
9. $3 \times 300 =$ _____
10. $11 \times 700 =$ _____

11. $4000 \times 7 =$ _____
12. $5 \times 8000 =$ _____
13. $8 \times 2000 =$ _____
14. $7 \times 3000 =$ _____
15. $11 \times 4000 =$ _____
16. $6 \times 600 =$ _____
17. $9 \times 60 =$ _____
18. $4000 \times 5 =$ _____
19. $7 \times 800 =$ _____
20. $8 \times 4000 =$ _____

THINK IT THROUGH

Which are worth the most: 35 nickels, 20 dimes, or 7 quarters?

2

LESSON 24   TACK ON TRAILING ZEROS

50 X 300

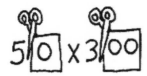

5|0 x 3|00

5 x 3 = 15

15|0||00|

You can multiply this quickly
in your head.
Just follow these steps:

- Cut off the trailing zeros.

- Multiply the remaining numbers.

- Collect ALL the zeros and tack
  them onto your answer.

Here's how a
mental-math
pro thinks . . .

400 x 30
4 x 3 = 12
12,000◄

TRY THESE IN YOUR HEAD.
Tack on ALL the trailing zeros.

1. 20 × 50   **3.** 300 × 300   **7.** 50 × 50

2. 400 × 90   **4.** 80 × 900   **8.** 70 × 3000

                  5. 60 × 200   **9.** 60 × 70

                  6. 7000 × 500   **10.** 120 × 40

POWER BUILDER A

1. $10 \times 10 =$ _____
2. $20 \times 20 =$ _____
3. $40 \times 50 =$ _____
4. $90 \times 90 =$ _____
5. $60 \times 70 =$ _____
6. $500 \times 20 =$ _____
7. $30 \times 400 =$ _____
8. $900 \times 10 =$ _____
9. $50 \times 500 =$ _____
10. $700 \times 80 =$ _____

11. $500 \times 500 =$ _____
12. $300 \times 700 =$ _____
13. $800 \times 100 =$ _____
14. $100 \times 100 =$ _____
15. $900 \times 900 =$ _____
16. $10 \times 2000 =$ _____
17. $20 \times 8000 =$ _____
18. $5000 \times 60 =$ _____
19. $80 \times 4000 =$ _____
20. $800 \times 1000 =$ _____

THINK IT THROUGH

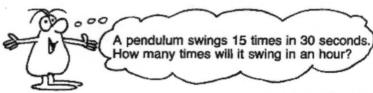

A pendulum swings 15 times in 30 seconds. How many times will it swing in an hour?

MENTAL MATH IN THE MIDDLE GRADES | LESSON 24   TACK ON TRAILING ZEROS

POWER BUILDER B

1. $40 \times 40 =$ _____
2. $30 \times 20 =$ _____
3. $40 \times 70 =$ _____
4. $80 \times 80 =$ _____
5. $90 \times 70 =$ _____
6. $200 \times 50 =$ _____
7. $40 \times 300 =$ _____
8. $800 \times 10 =$ _____
9. $30 \times 300 =$ _____
10. $800 \times 70 =$ _____

11. $600 \times 600 =$ _____
12. $700 \times 300 =$ _____
13. $500 \times 100 =$ _____
14. $200 \times 100 =$ _____
15. $800 \times 800 =$ _____
16. $20 \times 2000 =$ _____
17. $80 \times 2000 =$ _____
18. $6000 \times 50 =$ _____
19. $40 \times 8000 =$ _____
20. $700 \times 1000 =$ _____

THINK IT THROUGH

My heart beats 20 times in 15 seconds. How many times will it beat in an hour?

84

LESSON 25   FRONT-END MULTIPLYING $+$ $-$ $\times$ $\div$

$$\begin{array}{r} 52 \\ \times\ 7 \\ \hline \end{array}$$

Can you multiply this in your head?

It's easy if you break up one factor into smaller parts. Like this . . .

BREAK UP 52 . . . $52 \rightarrow 50 + 2$

MULTIPLY THE PARTS,
STARTING AT THE LEFT . . . $\times\ \ \ 7$

ADD . . . $350 + 14 = 364$

SO . . . $7 \times 52 = 364$

MENTAL MATH TIP ⟹

Think of it as multiplying from the left.

$$\begin{array}{r} 5\ 2 \\ \times\ 7 \end{array}$$

TRY THESE IN YOUR HEAD.
Multiply from the left.

1. 15×7
2. 23×5
3. 36×8
4. 3×54
5. 16×8
6. 31×4
7. 3×28
8. 7×27
9. 85×50
10. 20×28

POWER BUILDER A

1. $31 \times 7 =$ _____
2. $41 \times 3 =$ _____
3. $4 \times 22 =$ _____
4. $3 \times 83 =$ _____
5. $5 \times 51 =$ _____
6. $6 \times 83 =$ _____
7. $8 \times 94 =$ _____
8. $5 \times 58 =$ _____
9. $2 \times 78 =$ _____
10. $56 \times 2 =$ _____

11. $8 \times 58 =$ _____
12. $6 \times 66 =$ _____
13. $4 \times 48 =$ _____
14. $2 \times 96 =$ _____
15. $7 \times 77 =$ _____
16. $2 \times 59 =$ _____
17. $7 \times 51 =$ _____
18. $30 \times 41 =$ _____
19. $25 \times 30 =$ _____
20. $55 \times 40 =$ _____

THINK IT THROUGH

Which two different whole numbers that add to 20 will give the largest product?

MENTAL MATH IN THE MIDDLE GRADES   LESSON 25   FRONT-END MULTIPLYING

POWER BUILDER B

1. $21 \times 7 =$ _____
2. $41 \times 2 =$ _____
3. $3 \times 22 =$ _____
4. $2 \times 84 =$ _____
5. $4 \times 51 =$ _____
6. $6 \times 74 =$ _____
7. $9 \times 83 =$ _____
8. $65 \times 5 =$ _____
9. $87 \times 2 =$ _____
10. $55 \times 3 =$ _____

11. $4 \times 45 =$ _____
12. $5 \times 55 =$ _____
13. $5 \times 58 =$ _____
14. $2 \times 76 =$ _____
15. $6 \times 96 =$ _____
16. $2 \times 48 =$ _____
17. $6 \times 57 =$ _____
18. $30 \times 52 =$ _____
19. $20 \times 25 =$ _____
20. $45 \times 50 =$ _____

THINK IT THROUGH

Which two odd numbers that add to 20 will give the smallest product?

36

LESSON 26   FRONT-END MULTIPLYING

MULTIPLY IN YOUR HEAD

625
× 4

625? But how can I work with such a large number in my head?

EASY. Break it up into smaller parts.

Like this . . .

BREAK UP 625 . . .   600 + 25

MULTIPLY THE PARTS FROM THE LEFT . . .   × 4

ADD . . .   2400 + 100 = 2500

Now try this one.
How will you break up 423?

423
× 3

TRY THESE IN YOUR HEAD.
Multiply from the left.

1. 8 × 625   3. 112 × 8   7. 4 × 521
2. 4 × 256   4. 5 × 125   8. 3 × 252
                5. 525 × 2   9. 507 × 8
                6. 611 × 4   10. 7 × 911

POWER BUILDER A

1. 2 × 434 = _____
2. 121 × 5 = _____
3. 4 × 124 = _____
4. 135 × 2 = _____
5. 325 × 3 = _____
6. 7 × 303 = _____
7. 9 × 209 = _____
8. 801 × 6 = _____
9. 505 × 5 = _____
10. 9 × 111 = _____

11. 2 × 435 = _____
12. 165 × 5 = _____
13. 188 × 5 = _____
14. 525 × 8 = _____
15. 4 × 256 = _____
16. 123 × 3 = _____
17. 525 × 4 = _____
18. 4 × 625 = _____
19. 5 × 808 = _____
20. 505 × 6 = _____

THINK IT THROUGH

Pick three two-digit numbers.
Multiply each number by 101.
What pattern do you notice?

MENTAL MATH IN THE MIDDLE GRADES   LESSON 26   FRONT-END MULTIPLYING

POWER BUILDER B

1. 2 × 344 = _____
2. 122 × 5 = _____
3. 4 × 123 = _____
4. 148 × 2 = _____
5. 425 × 3 = _____
6. 404 × 7 = _____
7. 309 × 4 = _____
8. 6 × 801 = _____
9. 5 × 705 = _____
10. 519 × 2 = _____

11. 2 × 345 = _____
12. 145 × 5 = _____
13. 166 × 5 = _____
14. 425 × 8 = _____
15. 4 × 255 = _____
16. 3 × 213 = _____
17. 505 × 4 = _____
18. 3 × 423 = _____
19. 235 × 2 = _____
20. 9 × 311 = _____

THINK IT THROUGH

Study these problems: 114 × 1001 = 114,114
236 × 1001 = 236,236
Use the pattern to multiply these:
472 × 1001   203 × 1001   47 × 1001

38

LESSON 27   NOTICING NINES

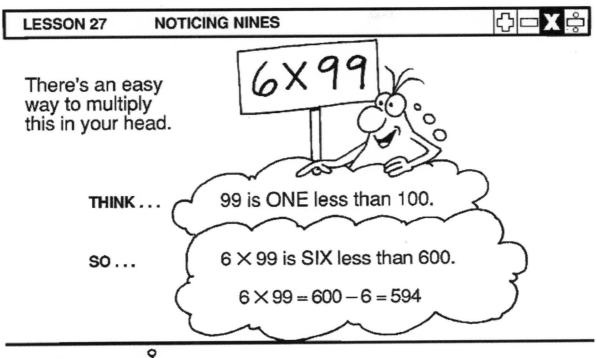

There's an easy way to multiply this in your head.

6 X 99

THINK ...   99 is ONE less than 100.

SO ...   6 × 99 is SIX less than 600.

$6 \times 99 = 600 - 6 = 594$

This is a good strategy to use with prices.

At $8.99 each, what would 6 robots cost?

Figure it out in your head!

TRY THESE IN YOUR HEAD.
Clean up the 9's, then adjust.

1. 8 × 99   **3.** 19 × 6   **7.** 15 at $1.99
2. 7 × 199   **4.** 29 × 5   **8.** 4 at $0.99
                     5. 6 at $4.99   **9.** 3 at $2.49
                     6. 3 at $1.49   **10.** 8 at $3.99

POWER BUILDER A

1. $4 \times 79 =$ _____
2. $8 \times 79 =$ _____
3. $3 \times 79 =$ _____
4. $6 \times 79 =$ _____
5. $2 \times 79 =$ _____
6. $8 \times 199 =$ _____
7. $6 \times 399 =$ _____
8. $5 \times 599 =$ _____
9. $3 \times 799 =$ _____
10. $2 \times 1999 =$ _____

11. $5 \times \$7.99 =$ _____
12. $2 \times \$39.99 =$ _____
13. $4 \times \$11.99 =$ _____
14. $3 \times \$19.99 =$ _____
15. $7 \times \$7.99 =$ _____
16. $3 \times \$2.99 =$ _____
17. $5 \times \$19.99 =$ _____
18. $4 \times \$1.99 =$ _____
19. $15 \times \$3.99 =$ _____
20. $5 \times \$49.99 =$ _____

THINK IT THROUGH

What is the mystery number? Clue: If you subtract the mystery number from 1000, you get a difference that is equal to 3 times 199.

MENTAL MATH IN THE MIDDLE GRADES   LESSON 27   NOTICING NINES

POWER BUILDER B

1. $8 \times 39 =$ _____
2. $6 \times 59 =$ _____
3. $4 \times 89 =$ _____
4. $5 \times 79 =$ _____
5. $7 \times 29 =$ _____
6. $8 \times 29 =$ _____
7. $6 \times 499 =$ _____
8. $5 \times 699 =$ _____
9. $3 \times 899 =$ _____
10. $3 \times 2999 =$ _____

11. $6 \times \$3.99 =$ _____
12. $3 \times \$19.99 =$ _____
13. $2 \times \$59.99 =$ _____
14. $7 \times \$1.99 =$ _____
15. $4 \times \$6.99 =$ _____
16. $6 \times \$1.99 =$ _____
17. $3 \times \$9.99 =$ _____
18. $5 \times \$29.99 =$ _____
19. $2 \times \$17.99 =$ _____
20. $25 \times \$1.99 =$ _____

THINK IT THROUGH

What is the mystery number? Clue: The mystery number is twice as much as 2 times 49.

UNIT THREE REVIEW   (CLASS DISCUSSION)

Mental Math Techniques
• **THINK QUARTERS.**
$550 + 125 + 50 = ?$
• **CLEAN UP 8'S AND 9'S.**
TO ADD . . . $198 + 499 = ?$
TO SUBTRACT . . . $672 - 98 = ?$
TO MULTIPLY . . . $7 \times \$3.99 = ?$
• **TACK ON TRAILING ZEROS.**
$9 \times 100 = ?$ $60 \times 400 = ?$
• **MULTIPLY FROM THE LEFT.**
$8 \times 23 = ?$ $253 \times 4 = ?$

Do the problems below in your head. Tell which techniques you find useful for each one.

1. 4×399
2. 508×4
3. $\$3.47 + \$1.99$
4. $425 + 75 + 75$
5. 7×400
6. $733 - 299$
7. $247 + 399$
8. $5 \times \$19.99$
9. 200×900
10. 213×3

Talk about each problem below. What's an easy way to do it in your head? Tell how you would think it through.

1. $574 - 98$
2. $275 + 50 + 25$
3. 5×60
4. 8×425
5. $\$45.00 - \$14.99$
6. 5×130

7. $98 + 140$
8. $20 \times \$1.99$
9. $150 + 125$
10. 30×30
11. 8×69
12. 50×800

UNIT 3 PROGRESS TEST

1. 50 × 50 = _____

2. 3 × 424 = _____

3. 199 + 45 = _____

4. 79 + 25 = _____

5. 75 − 39 = _____

6. 125 + 50 = _____

7. 6 × 40 = _____

8. $54.99 + $3.25 = _____

9. 3000 × 5 = _____

10. 40 × 70 = _____

11. 4 × 26 = _____

12. 8 × 600 = _____

13. 50 + 25 + 75 = _____

14. 73 × 5 = _____

15. 98 + 67 = _____

16. 6 × 806 = _____

17. 95 − 29 = _____

18. 215 + 98 = _____

19. 8 × 625 = _____

20. 5275 − 1999 = _____

21. 225 + 50 + 50 = _____

22. 200 × 11 = _____

23. 5 × $2.99 = _____

24. $10.00 − $5.98 = _____

25. 255 × 2 = _____

26. 325 + 50 + 25 = _____

27. 900 × 6 = _____

28. $4.98 + $8.99 = _____

29. 100 × 6 = _____

30. 50 × 7 = _____

31. 12 × 300 = _____

32. 299 + 81 = _____

33. 3 × $2.49 = _____

34. $45.99 + $9.99 = _____

35. 149 + 45 = _____

36. 9 × 1000 = _____

37. 625 + 50 + 125 = _____

38. $20.00 − $13.98 = _____

39. 4019 + 298 = _____

40. 8 × 599 = _____

Perfect Squares: Do you KNOW THEM by heart?

We call them "Perfect Squares" because we can draw them as squares.

See how they line up along the main diagonal in your Count-By table.

MEMORIZE them all, from 1*1 to 10*10:

1	2	3	4	5	6	7	8	9	10
2	4	6	8	10	12	14	16	18	20
3	6	9	12	15	18	21	24	27	30
4	8	12	16	20	24	28	32	36	40
5	10	15	20	25	30	35	40	45	50
6	12	18	24	30	36	42	48	54	60
7	14	21	28	35	42	49	56	63	70
8	16	24	32	40	48	56	64	72	80
9	18	27	36	45	54	63	72	81	90
10	20	30	40	50	60	70	80	90	100

1, 4, 9, 16, 25, 36, 49, 64, 81, 100

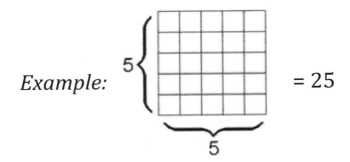

Example: = 25

Using Perfect Squares

We call them "Perfect Squares" because we can put them in squares like in the pictures we have seen above. See also how they are lined up along the main diagonal in your Count-By table. The list of perfect squares: **1, 4, 9, 16, 25, 36, 49, 64, 72, 81, 100** is a very important one and should be mastered. We can use it for answering multiplication questions, as we do in the next drill.

- If 6*6 is 36, then what is 7*6? _____
- If 5*5 is 25, then what is 6*5? _____
- If 4*4 is 16, then what is 5*4? _____
- If 8*8 is 64, then what is 7*8? _____
- If 8*8 is 64, then what is 9*8? _____
- If 6*6 is 36, then what is 5*6? _____
- If 9*9 is 81, then what is 8*9? _____
- If 7*7 is 49, then what is 8*7? _____
- If 7*7 is 49, then what is 6*7? _____
- If 7*7 is 49, then what is 7*8? _____
- If 8*8 is 64, then what is 8*7? _____
- If 6*6 is 36, then what is 6*5? _____
- If 9*9 is 81, then what is 9*8? _____

Note to Parent

- Reinforce the idea that if we know the PERFECT SQUARE, we can use it to answer other multiplication questions when the numbers are one apart.

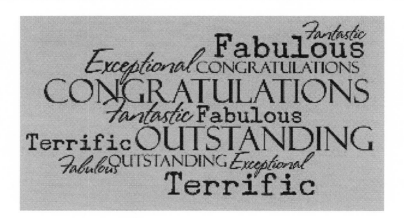

Class Activity: Rounding

A. Round each of the following numbers to the nearest TEN:

14 ___	58 ___	73 ___	98 ___
75 ___	153 ___	278 ___	95 ___
94 ___	88 ___	171 ___	9 ___
104 ___	102 ___	5 ___	4 ___
194 ___	297 ___	355 ___	444 ___

B. Round each number to the nearest HUNDRED:

514 ___	558 ___	373 ___	198 ___
375 ___	150 ___	278 ___	95 ___
94 ___	88 ___	171 ___	29 ___
104 ___	702 ___	500 ___	4 ___
891 ___	249 ___	955 ___	444 ___

C. Give an example for a number that when rounded to the nearest TEN and when rounded to the nearest HUNDRED you get the same result. _____

D. Give an example for a number that when rounded to the nearest HUNDRED and when rounded to the nearest THOUSAND you get the same result. _____

E. Give an example for a number that when rounded to the nearest TEN, HUNDRED and THOUSAND you get the same result. _____

Round each of the following numbers as indicated

	To nearest 10	To nearest 100	To nearest 1,000
1,431			
2,679			
3,111			
456			
789			
501			
9,310			
8,750			
1,500			
2,450			
5,945			
2,601			
3			
996			
51			
5,555			

ORDER OF OPERATIONS

How to do a math problem with more than one operation in the correct order.

1. BRACKETS
2. MULTIPLICATION and DIVISION
3. ADDITION and SUBTRACTION

A. Solve

1. 5×3-6
2. 5+3×6
3. (5+3)×6
4. 5×(7-3)+2
5. (5+14+2) ÷ (3+4)

6. 15-4×2
7. (15-4) ×7-10
8. 40÷8-3
9. 40÷(8-3)
10. 40÷5+10÷2

11. (4+15÷3) ×6
12. ((4+14)÷3+2) ×6
13. (26+(14+3)×2) ÷6
14. ((15-4) ×(10-7)) ÷3
15. 40÷(5+3) ×2

B. Insert the correct operations (+, -, ÷ or ×) into the empty boxes, and USE BRACKETS were necessary to make the two sides equal to one another

1. 1 ☐ 2 ☐ 3 ☐ 4 = 0
2. 1 ☐ 2 ☐ 3 ☐ 4 = 1
3. 1 ☐ 2 ☐ 3 ☐ 4 = 2
4. 1 ☐ 2 ☐ 3 ☐ 4 = 3
5. 1 ☐ 2 ☐ 3 ☐ 4 = 4

6. 1 ☐ 2 ☐ 3 ☐ 4 = 5
7. 1 ☐ 2 ☐ 3 ☐ 4 = 21
8. 1 ☐ 2 ☐ 3 ☐ 4 = 28
9. 1 ☐ 2 ☐ 3 ☐ 4 = 9
10. 1 ☐ 2 ☐ 3 ☐ 4 = 10 (find 3 different ways)

C. Insert the correct operations (+, -, ÷ or ×) into the empty boxes to make a true equation

1. 48☐8☐4 = 10
2. 9☐5☐(2☐3) = 14
3. (16☐4)☐(63☐3) = 84
4. 8☐3☐1☐5 = 6
5. 7☐(5☐2)☐1 = 49

6. 4☐5☐1 = 8
7. 40☐5☐1 = 8
8. 4☐5☐1 = 19
9. 64☐8☐4☐3 = 7
10. 64☐8☐4☐3 = 5

RENERT'S **BRIGHT** MINDS

D. **Four 4s** - Make all the numbers from 0 to 20 by using four 4s ONLY. Two of them are already solved for you as examples. You may "glue" two of the 4s and use them as the number 44.

0=4+4-4-4	5=	10=	15=
1=	6=	11=	16=
2=	7=44÷4-4	12=	17=
3=	8=	13=	18=
4=	9=	14=	19=
			20=

E. **Three 3s** – How many different numbers can you make by using three 3s? You may "glue" two of the 3s and use them as the number 33. Make sure to use order of operations and brackets correctly.

Four Dice:

□ □ □ □

Make all the numbers from 0 to 20 by using these four numbers ONLY. You MUST use each of the numbers once. You may use +, -, ×, ÷, and also POWERS.

0=	5=	10=	15=
1=	6=	11=	16=
2=	7=	12=	17=
3=	8=	13=	18=
4=	9=	14=	19=
			20=

Four Dice:

☐ ☐ ☐ ☐

Make all the numbers from 0 to 20 by using these four numbers ONLY. You MUST use each of the numbers once. You may use +, -, ×, ÷, and also POWERS.

0=	5=	10=	15=
1=	6=	11=	16=
2=	7=	12=	17=
3=	8=	13=	18=
4=	9=	14=	19=
			20=

Three Dice:

☐ ☐ ☐

Make all the numbers from 0 to 20 by using these three numbers ONLY. You MUST use each of the numbers once. You may use +, -, ×, ÷, and also POWERS.

0=	5=	10=	15=
1=	6=	11=	16=
2=	7=	12=	17=
3=	8=	13=	18=
4=	9=	14=	19=
			20=

Three Dice:

□ □ □

Make all the numbers from 0 to 20 by using these three numbers ONLY. You MUST use each of the numbers once. You may use +, -, ×, ÷, and also POWERS.

0=	5=	10=	15=
1=	6=	11=	16=
2=	7=	12=	17=
3=	8=	13=	18=
4=	9=	14=	19=
			20=

3D Solids and 2D Shapes – KNOW their names

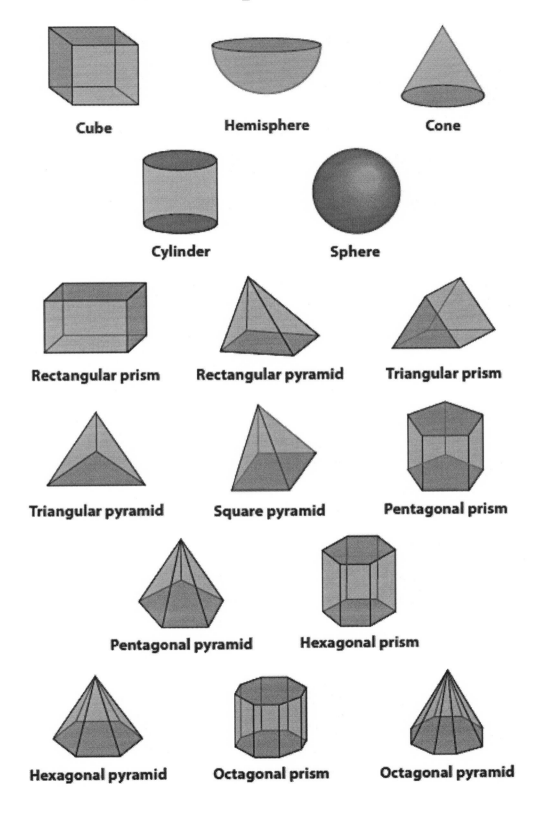

Cube

Hemisphere

Cone

Cylinder

Sphere

Rectangular prism

Rectangular pyramid

Triangular prism

Triangular pyramid

Square pyramid

Pentagonal prism

Pentagonal pyramid

Hexagonal prism

Hexagonal pyramid

Octagonal prism

Octagonal pyramid

Prisms vs. Pyramids

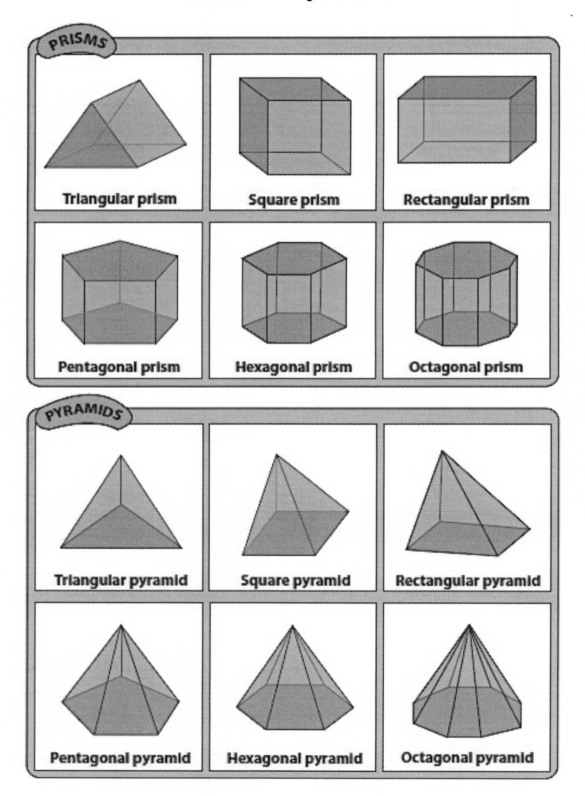

PRISMS

Triangular prism	**Square prism**	**Rectangular prism**
Pentagonal prism	**Hexagonal prism**	**Octagonal prism**

PYRAMIDS

Triangular pyramid	**Square pyramid**	**Rectangular pyramid**
Pentagonal pyramid	**Hexagonal pyramid**	**Octagonal pyramid**

Nets of Solids

Match the net to the solid

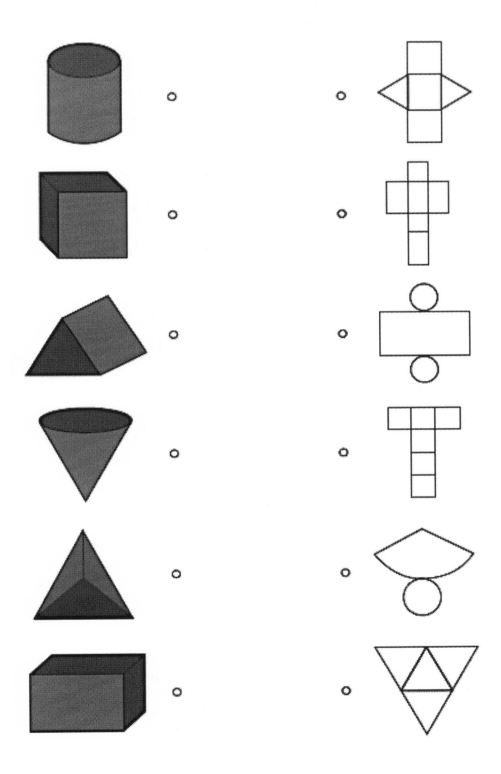

Nets of Solids

Choose for each solid the net that represents it

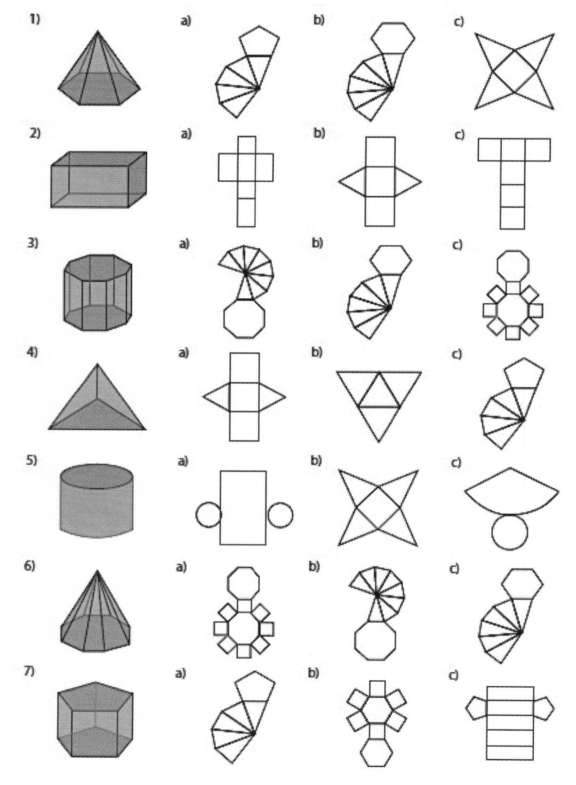

1) a) b) c)

2) a) b) c)

3) a) b) c)

4) a) b) c)

5) a) b) c)

6) a) b) c)

7) a) b) c)

Vertices-Edges-Faces

- Count for each solid the number of Faces, Edges and Vertices
  - Calculate for each solid **Vertices + Faces - Edges**
    - **What do you observe?**

1)

Faces ☐

Edges ☐

Vertices ☐

Name: _____

2)

Faces ☐

Edges ☐

Vertices ☐

Name: _____

3)

Faces ☐

Edges ☐

Vertices ☐

Name: _____

4)

Faces ☐

Edges ☐

Vertices ☐

Name: _____

5)

Faces ☐

Edges ☐

Vertices ☐

Name: _____

6)

Faces ☐

Edges ☐

Vertices ☐

Name: _____

7)

Faces ☐

Edges ☐

Vertices ☐

Name: _____

8)

Faces ☐

Edges ☐

Vertices ☐

Name: _____

More on FRACTIONS!

An **IMPROPER FRACTION** is a fraction in which the numerator is bigger than the denominator **(Top>Bottom)**. Such fractions are bigger than a whole. These are all examples of improper fractions: $\frac{5}{2}$, $\frac{14}{5}$, $\frac{7}{4}$, $\frac{101}{23}$

A **MIXED NUMBER** is a number that has a whole number part and a fraction part. These are all examples of mixed numbers: $3\frac{5}{2}$, $7\frac{4}{5}$, $20\frac{1}{4}$, $6\frac{21}{23}$

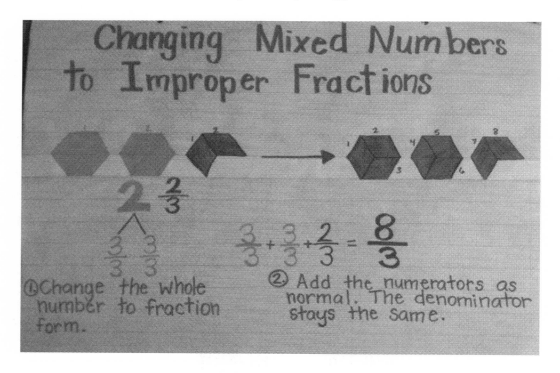

Changing Improper Fractions to Mixed Numbers

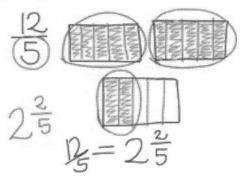

Write each amount as a mixed number.

1)

2)

3)

4)

5)

Write each amount as an improper fraction.

6)

7)

8)

9)

10)

11)

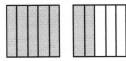

Write each as mixed number, and ALSO as an improper fraction.

1) 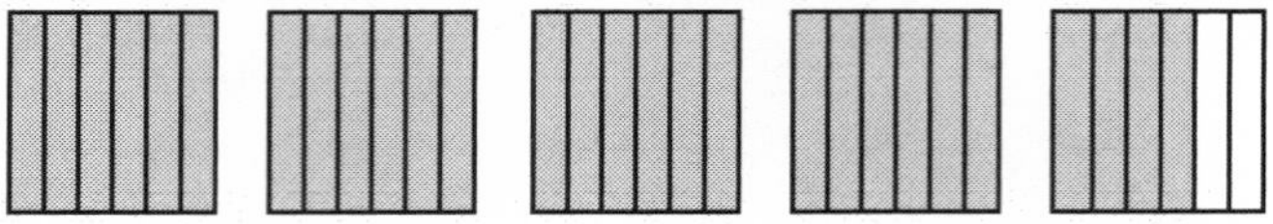

2) 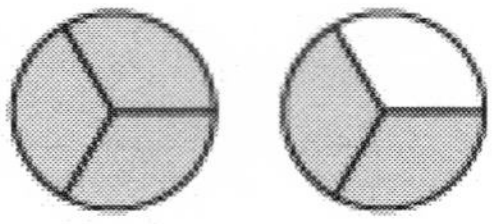

3) 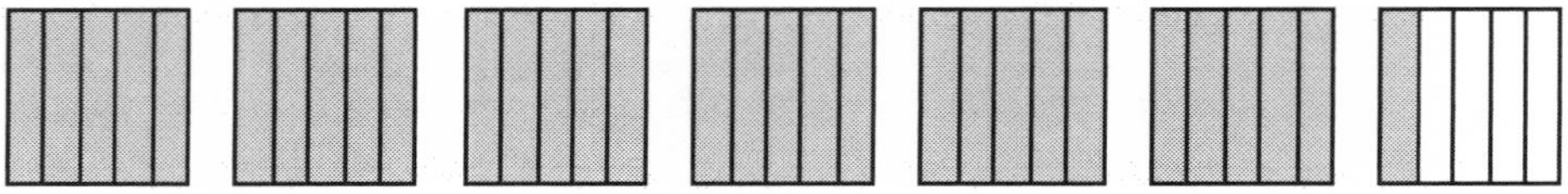

4) 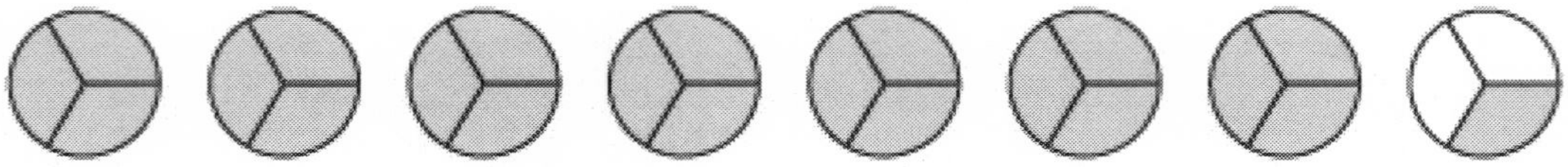

5) 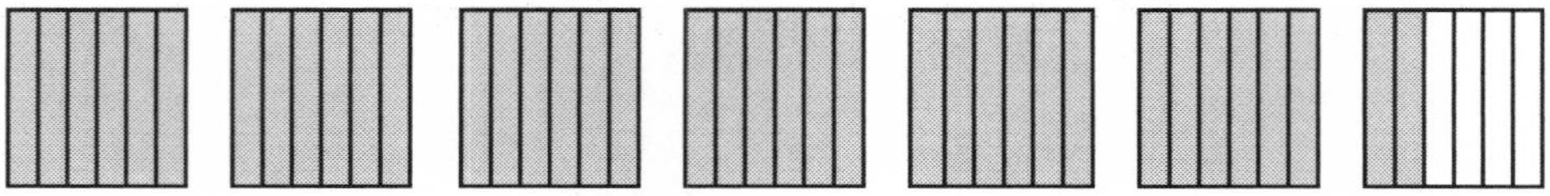

Write each as mixed number, and ALSO as an improper fraction.

6) 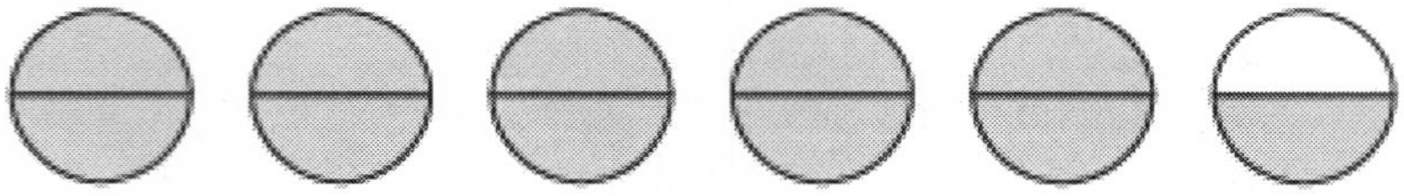

7) 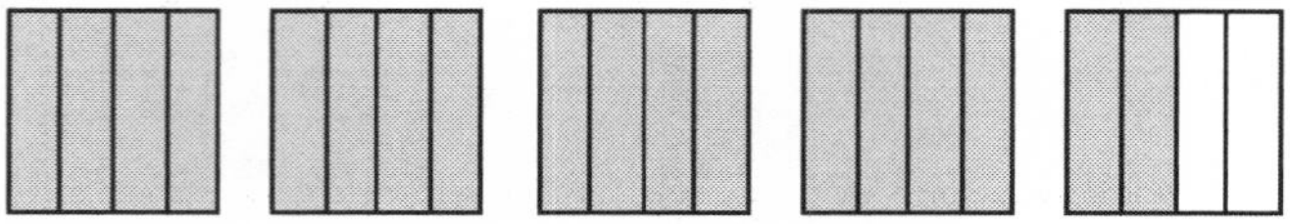

8) 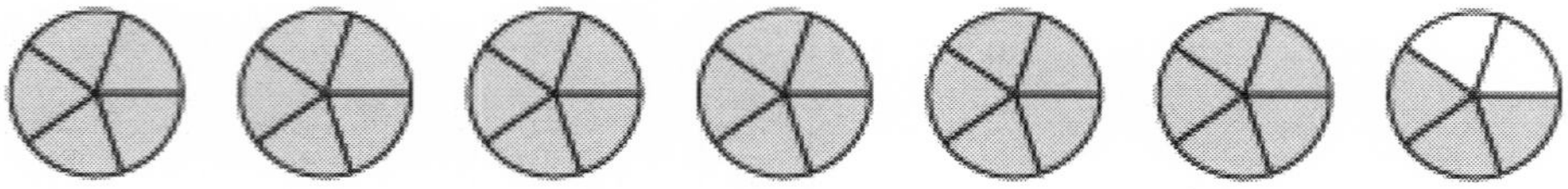

9) 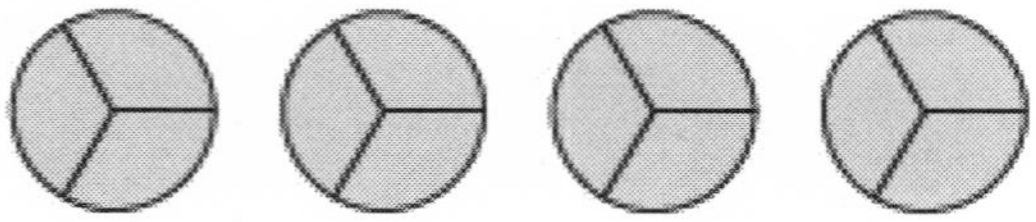

10) 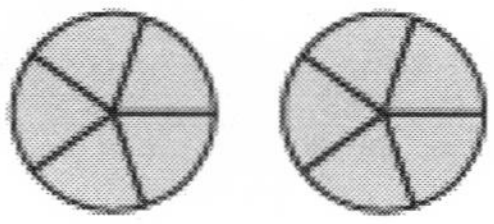

CONVERT from a mixed number to an improper fraction.

a) $2\frac{1}{2}$ = [   ]

b) $8\frac{1}{3}$ = [   ]

c) $1\frac{2}{5}$ = [   ]

d) $3\frac{5}{7}$ = [   ]

e) $4\frac{2}{3}$ = [   ]

f) $2\frac{1}{4}$ = [   ]

g) $3\frac{1}{4}$ = [   ]

h) $1\frac{2}{3}$ = [   ]

i) $10\frac{1}{2}$ = [   ]

j) $2\frac{3}{5}$ = [   ]

k) $6\frac{4}{5}$ = [   ]

l) $1\frac{3}{4}$ = [   ]

CONVERT from a mixed number to an improper fraction.

Ex) $6 \frac{1}{5} = \frac{31}{5}$

1) $10 \frac{1}{4} =$

2) $10 \frac{1}{6} =$

3) $6 \frac{2}{6} =$

4) $3 \frac{1}{7} =$

5) $1 \frac{2}{5} =$

6) $4 \frac{1}{8} =$

7) $2 \frac{1}{6} =$

8) $10 \frac{4}{6} =$

9) $7 \frac{4}{6} =$

10) $8 \frac{6}{7} =$

11) $3 \frac{2}{5} =$

12) $6 \frac{2}{10} =$

13) $8 \frac{1}{9} =$

14) $2 \frac{1}{3} =$

15) $9 \frac{4}{6} =$

16) $2 \frac{1}{2} =$

17) $3 \frac{2}{3} =$

18) $5 \frac{2}{4} =$

19) $9 \frac{2}{8} =$

20) $8 \frac{1}{7} =$

CONVERT from an improper fraction to a mixed number.

a) $\dfrac{11}{7}$ = _____

b) $\dfrac{13}{8}$ = _____

c) $\dfrac{5}{2}$ = _____

d) $\dfrac{12}{5}$ = _____

e) $\dfrac{18}{7}$ = _____

f) $\dfrac{10}{9}$ = _____

g) $\dfrac{25}{3}$ = _____

h) $\dfrac{17}{6}$ = _____

i) $\dfrac{11}{4}$ = _____

j) $\dfrac{29}{7}$ = _____

k) $\dfrac{18}{3}$ = _____

l) $\dfrac{45}{4}$ = _____

CONVERT from an improper fraction to a mixed number.

Ex) $\dfrac{17}{2} = 8 \dfrac{1}{2}$

1) $\dfrac{13}{2} =$

2) $\dfrac{79}{9} =$

3) $\dfrac{35}{4} =$

4) $\dfrac{37}{5} =$

5) $\dfrac{13}{7} =$

6) $\dfrac{5}{2} =$

7) $\dfrac{28}{3} =$

8) $\dfrac{25}{3} =$

9) $\dfrac{65}{7} =$

10) $\dfrac{32}{6} =$

11) $\dfrac{36}{5} =$

12) $\dfrac{64}{7} =$

13) $\dfrac{12}{7} =$

14) $\dfrac{42}{5} =$

15) $\dfrac{79}{8} =$

16) $\dfrac{66}{7} =$

17) $\dfrac{68}{8} =$

18) $\dfrac{3}{2} =$

19) $\dfrac{19}{3} =$

20) $\dfrac{38}{4} =$

Fill in the Blanks - Mixed Number to Improper Fraction

Instruction: Fill in the blanks to complete the conversion between mixed numbers and improper fractions.

a) $\boxed{}$ = $\dfrac{9}{5}$

b) $\boxed{}$ = $\dfrac{5}{2}$

c) $\boxed{}$ = $\dfrac{5}{4}$

d) $10\dfrac{1}{3}$ = $\boxed{}$

e) $\boxed{}$ = $\dfrac{29}{10}$

f) $\boxed{}$ = $\dfrac{11}{4}$

g) $2\dfrac{7}{9}$ = $\boxed{}$

h) $2\dfrac{5}{8}$ = $\boxed{}$

i) $1\dfrac{4}{9}$ = $\boxed{}$

j) $14\dfrac{1}{2}$ = $\boxed{}$

k) $2\dfrac{8}{9}$ = $\boxed{}$

l) $\boxed{}$ = $\dfrac{8}{3}$

Mixed Numbers and Improper Fractions Conversion

Instruction: Convert mixed numbers into improper fractions, or improper fractions into mixed numbers.

a) $1\dfrac{1}{3}$ = [____]

b) $\dfrac{11}{5}$ = [____]

c) $\dfrac{17}{8}$ = [____]

d) $\dfrac{5}{3}$ = [____]

e) $\dfrac{6}{5}$ = [____]

f) $12\dfrac{1}{4}$ = [____]

g) $\dfrac{14}{3}$ = [____]

h) $2\dfrac{3}{8}$ = [____]

i) $\dfrac{14}{9}$ = [____]

j) $18\dfrac{1}{2}$ = [____]

k) $\dfrac{11}{4}$ = [____]

l) $1\dfrac{1}{4}$ = [____]

True or False - Improper Fractions and Mixed Numbers Conversion

Instruction: Check whether the conversion between improper fractions and mixed number is correct. Write TRUE or FALSE on the space provided.

a) $2\dfrac{7}{8} = \dfrac{21}{8}$

b) $2\dfrac{8}{9} = \dfrac{26}{9}$

c) $2\dfrac{5}{8} = \dfrac{21}{8}$

d) $1\dfrac{3}{4} = \dfrac{7}{4}$

e) $\dfrac{7}{4} = 1\dfrac{3}{4}$

f) $1\dfrac{1}{6} = \dfrac{5}{6}$

g) $\dfrac{17}{7} = 2\dfrac{3}{7}$

h) $\dfrac{17}{9} = 1\dfrac{8}{9}$

i) $\dfrac{19}{7} = 1\dfrac{4}{7}$

j) $\dfrac{4}{5} = 1\dfrac{2}{5}$

k) $2\dfrac{1}{3} = \dfrac{7}{3}$

l) $\dfrac{3}{5} = 1\dfrac{3}{10}$

Convert from improper fraction to a mixed number

Ex) $\dfrac{14}{3} = 4\dfrac{2}{3}$

1) $\dfrac{88}{9} =$

2) $\dfrac{53}{5} =$

3) $\dfrac{92}{9} =$

4) $\dfrac{46}{7} =$

5) $\dfrac{35}{6} =$

6) $\dfrac{13}{2} =$

7) $\dfrac{78}{8} =$

8) $\dfrac{37}{8} =$

9) $\dfrac{57}{9} =$

10) $\dfrac{9}{2} =$

11) $\dfrac{21}{2} =$

12) $\dfrac{29}{6} =$

13) $\dfrac{7}{2} =$

14) $\dfrac{34}{5} =$

15) $\dfrac{33}{7} =$

16) $\dfrac{69}{8} =$

17) $\dfrac{27}{6} =$

18) $\dfrac{65}{8} =$

19) $\dfrac{35}{4} =$

20) $\dfrac{58}{7} =$

Equal or Not Equal – Improper Fractions and Mixed Numbers Conversion

Instruction: Check whether the conversion between improper fraction and mixed number is correct. Write = or ≠ on the box between the fractions.

> **or** <

a) $2\frac{3}{5}$ ☐ $\frac{11}{10}$

b) $\frac{10}{7}$ ☐ $1\frac{3}{7}$

c) $\frac{3}{2}$ ☐ $1\frac{1}{2}$

d) $\frac{5}{2}$ ☐ $2\frac{1}{2}$

e) $2\frac{3}{5}$ ☐ $\frac{13}{5}$

f) $\frac{3}{2}$ ☐ $1\frac{1}{2}$

g) $\frac{20}{7}$ ☐ $2\frac{6}{7}$

h) $\frac{21}{10}$ ☐ $2\frac{1}{10}$

i) $1\frac{4}{7}$ ☐ $\frac{11}{7}$

j) $\frac{8}{3}$ ☐ $1\frac{1}{3}$

k) $1\frac{1}{6}$ ☐ $\frac{7}{6}$

l) $1\frac{1}{2}$ ☐ $\frac{3}{2}$

Arrange Similar Proper Fractions

Instruction: Arrange the fractions below from least to greatest. Write your answers on the blank boxes.

a)

$$\frac{17}{24} \qquad \frac{7}{24} \qquad \frac{19}{24} \qquad \frac{18}{24} \qquad \frac{20}{24}$$

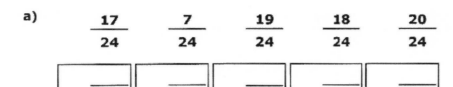

b)

$$\frac{2}{17} \qquad \frac{5}{17} \qquad \frac{8}{17} \qquad \frac{6}{17} \qquad \frac{17}{17}$$

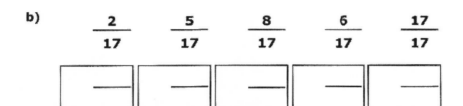

c)

$$\frac{5}{12} \qquad \frac{6}{12} \qquad \frac{8}{12} \qquad \frac{1}{12} \qquad \frac{9}{12}$$

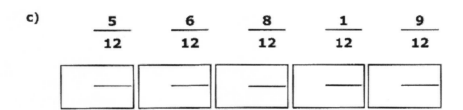

d)

$$\frac{12}{25} \qquad \frac{3}{25} \qquad \frac{17}{25} \qquad \frac{1}{25} \qquad \frac{5}{25}$$

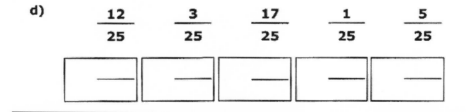

Arrange Similar Proper Fractions

Instruction: Arrange the fractions below from least to greatest. Write your answers on the blank boxes.

a)

$$\frac{17}{21} \qquad \frac{8}{21} \qquad \frac{18}{21} \qquad \frac{5}{21} \qquad \frac{9}{21}$$

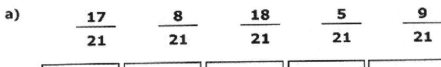

b)

$$\frac{9}{20} \qquad \frac{14}{20} \qquad \frac{16}{20} \qquad \frac{3}{20} \qquad \frac{5}{20}$$

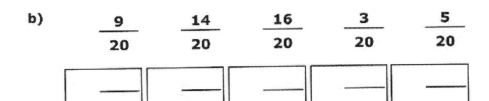

c)

$$\frac{6}{12} \qquad \frac{11}{12} \qquad \frac{8}{12} \qquad \frac{10}{12} \qquad \frac{7}{12}$$

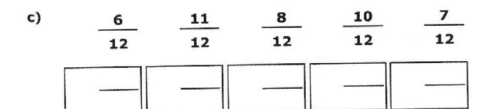

d)

$$\frac{13}{18} \qquad \frac{15}{18} \qquad \frac{17}{18} \qquad \frac{2}{18} \qquad \frac{8}{18}$$

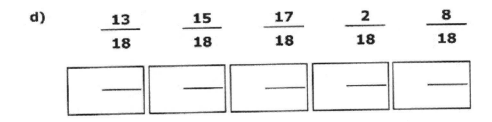

Arrange Similar Fractions and Mixed Numbers

Instruction: Arrange the fractions below from least to greatest. Write your answers on the blank boxes.

a)

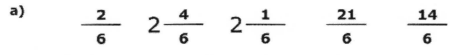

$$\frac{2}{6} \qquad 2\frac{4}{6} \qquad 2\frac{1}{6} \qquad \frac{21}{6} \qquad \frac{14}{6}$$

b)

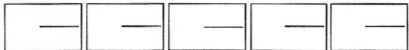

$$\frac{22}{15} \qquad \frac{8}{15} \qquad \frac{5}{15} \qquad \frac{20}{15} \qquad \frac{2}{15}$$

c)

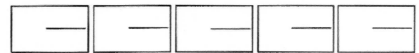

$$\frac{14}{24} \qquad \frac{2}{24} \qquad 1\frac{7}{24} \qquad \frac{20}{24} \qquad 1\frac{3}{24}$$

d)

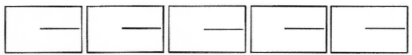

$$\frac{10}{18} \qquad \frac{13}{18} \qquad 1\frac{16}{18} \qquad \frac{12}{18} \qquad \frac{16}{18}$$

Arrange Similar Fractions and Mixed Numbers

Instruction: Arrange the fractions below from least to greatest. Write your answers on the blank boxes.

a)

$$\frac{10}{7} \qquad 4\frac{1}{7} \qquad 1\frac{6}{7} \qquad \frac{4}{7} \qquad \frac{3}{7}$$

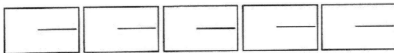

b)

$$1\frac{17}{18} \qquad 1\frac{12}{18} \qquad \frac{15}{18} \qquad \frac{16}{18} \qquad 1\frac{4}{18}$$

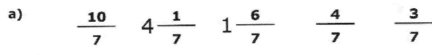

c)

$$\frac{23}{25} \qquad \frac{3}{25} \qquad \frac{1}{25} \qquad \frac{8}{25} \qquad 1\frac{5}{25}$$

d)

$$1\frac{15}{17} \qquad 1\frac{13}{17} \qquad \frac{7}{17} \qquad \frac{21}{17} \qquad \frac{29}{17}$$

Use the grid paper to perform LONG MULTIPLICATION

5 3	9 3	8 9	7 3	9 0
× 9	× 3	× 5	× 7	× 4

3 7	5 9	3 6	9 2	9 7
× 5	× 8	× 8	× 7	× 7

1 5	9 7	2 4	2 1	1 6
× 6	× 9	× 7	× 2	× 3

4 6	2 1	9 5	2 2	6 6
× 7	× 3	× 6	× 8	× 3

4 0	4 3	3 4	5 9	5 9
× 3	× 3	× 6	× 3	× 9

4 8	8 7	6 1	1 5	1 7
× 7	× 5	× 3	× 4	× 5

Use the grid paper to perform LONG MULTIPLICATION

```
  5 9 1        8 1 8        2 1 3        5 6 1
    × 3          × 6          × 9          × 6
```

```
  2 0 3        9 4 1        4 6 2        5 6 3
    × 9          × 7          × 3          × 4
```

```
  9 0 3        3 8 5        2 8 8        8 6 5
    × 5          × 4          × 3          × 4
```

```
  2 2 1        1 4 5        7 2 4        4 8 7
    × 5          × 9          × 6          × 7
```

```
  8 6 9        3 2 7        4 2 7        5 0 6
    × 4          × 8          × 9          × 6
```

```
  4 3 1        2 1 0        8 9 3        5 9 8
    × 5          × 7          × 6          × 7
```

Use the grid paper to perform LONG DIVISION

(1)
$$3 \overline{)165} = 55$$
15
15
15
0

(2)
$$7 \overline{)434}$$

(3)
$$2 \overline{)188}$$

(4)
$$9 \overline{)441}$$

(5)
$$4 \overline{)276}$$

(6)
$$8 \overline{)752}$$

(7)
$$5 \overline{)345}$$

(8)
$$6 \overline{)114}$$

(9)
$$3 \overline{)237}$$

(10)
$$9 \overline{)333}$$

(11)
$$7 \overline{)693}$$

(12)
$$5 \overline{)215}$$

(13)
$$4 \overline{)228}$$

(14)
$$2 \overline{)148}$$

(15)
$$8 \overline{)152}$$

(16)
$$6 \overline{)546}$$

(17)
$$7 \overline{)665}$$

(18)
$$5 \overline{)335}$$

(19)
$$4 \overline{)232}$$

(20)
$$2 \overline{)178}$$

(21)
$$9 \overline{)135}$$

(22)
$$3 \overline{)138}$$

(23)
$$8 \overline{)392}$$

(24)
$$6 \overline{)126}$$

(25)
$$3 \overline{)216}$$

Use the grid paper to perform LONG DIVISION

(1) 5 ⟌ 4,3,3,5

(2) 7 ⟌ 1,9,8,8

(3) 3 ⟌ 2,8,8,9

(4) 4 ⟌ 3,1,5,2

(5) 2 ⟌ 1,6,3,2

(6) 6 ⟌ 3,9,7,2

(7) 9 ⟌ 4,6,4,4

(8) 8 ⟌ 2,9,6,8

(9) 4 ⟌ 1,1,4,8

(10) 3 ⟌ 2,6,5,5

(11) 7 ⟌ 1,6,3,8

(12) 9 ⟌ 4,3,1,1

(13) 6 ⟌ 3,9,7,8

(14) 2 ⟌ 1,9,6,6

(15) 5 ⟌ 1,4,6,5

(16) 8 ⟌ 7,1,6,8

(17) 6 ⟌ 3,1,6,2

(18) 4 ⟌ 3,8,3,6

(19) 8 ⟌ 5,3,9,2

(20) 5 ⟌ 4,6,8,5

Use the grid paper to perform LONG DIVISION

(1) 4) 1 6 9

(2) 8) 5 4 6

(3) 3) 1 8 4

(4) 9) 6 7 3

(5) 5) 3 8 7

(6) 7) 4 5 3

(7) 2) 1 5 7

(8) 6) 5 6 7

(9) 5) 3 7 8

(10) 8) 2 3 5

(11) 3) 1 1 2

(12) 7) 6 2 8

(13) 4) 1 4 6

(14) 2) 1 6 5

(15) 6) 4 5 8

(16) 9) 1 0 3

(17) 7) 5 8 9

(18) 2) 1 9 5

(19) 8) 7 5 5

(20) 3) 2 8 3

(21) 9) 8 7 6

(22) 5) 2 6 8

(23) 6) 5 8 4

(24) 4) 1 3 0

(25) 7) 5 5 4

Use the grid paper to perform LONG DIVISION

(1) 2) 1,3,9,3

(2) 8) 1,5,5,0

(3) 6) 4,4,9,8

(4) 9) 2,5,9,0

(5) 7) 2,8,8,6

(6) 3) 2,9,9,5

(7) 4) 2,9,5,0

(8) 5) 3,6,7,6

(9) 2) 1,5,7,9

(10) 9) 6,8,1,7

(11) 8) 7,6,6,9

(12) 3) 1,8,3,4

(13) 4) 3,4,1,8

(14) 7) 1,9,0,0

(15) 5) 2,6,2,7

(16) 6) 2,3,7,7

Division Piece-by-Piece

REMEMBER that A÷B means "How many times B goes into A". For instance 6÷2 is 3 because 2 goes into 6 three times. You can figure this out if you count by 2s: 2, 4, 6. For the same reason 31÷5 is 6 with remainder 1 because we can squeeze six 5s into 30, and then we still have 1 left. If you are not sure how many 5s go into 31, use your Count By 5s: 5, 10, 15, 20, 25, 30... so six of them, with a remainder of 1.

When dividing bigger numbers, the trick is to break them into "good" pieces that are easy to work with. Let us practice division by 3, so you can see it better. When we divide by 3, all the numbers that are on the Count By 3s list are good for us: **3, 6, 9, 12, 15, 18, 21, 24, 27, 30**

All these numbers multiplied by 10 are also good for us:

30, 60, 90, 120, 150, 180, 210, 240, 270, 300

So now let us try to divide 435 by 3. Doing it all at once in our heads is difficult; so let's break the 435 into pieces that are easy to divide by 3.

For example: 435÷3 = (300 + 120 + 15)÷3
Now ask: How many 3s go into 300? How many go into 120? How many go into 15?
Answer: 100 + 40 + 5 = 145

Another example: 835÷3 = (300 + 300 + 210 + 25)÷3
Now ask: How many 3s go into 300? How many go into 210? How may go into 25?
Answer: 100 + 100 + 70 + 8 (remainder 1) = 278 R1

Now try to divide the following numbers by 3 on your own: remember that the key is to break the numbers into pieces that are easy to divide by 3 from the lists above.

127÷3   347÷3   738÷3

196÷3   457÷3   938÷3

Dividing by 5 Piece-by-Piece

When dividing by 5, the "good" numbers for us are the ones on the Count By 5s list:

5, 10, 15, 20, 25, 30, 35, 40, 45, 50

Each of these numbers with a 0 at the end is also good for us:

50, 100, 150, 200, 250, 300, 350, 400, 450, 500

Each of these numbers with two zeros at the end is still good for us:

500, 1000, 1500, 2000, 2500, 3000, 3500, 4000, 4500, 5000

Let us do a couple of examples, and then you do a few on your own:

For example: 735÷5.
Break the 735 into 500 + 200 + 35.
Now ask: How many 5s go into 500? How many go into 200? How many go into 35?
Answer: 100 + 40 + 7 = 147

Another example: 2,817÷5.

Break the 2,817 into 2,000 + 500 + 300 + 17.

Now ask: How many 5s go into 2,000? How many go into 500? How may go into 300? How many 5s go into 17? Answer: 400 + 100 + 60 + 3 (remainder 2) = 563 R2

Now try to divide the following numbers by 5 on your own: remember that the key is to break the numbers into pieces that are easy to divide by 5 from the lists above.

127÷5   347÷5   738÷5

196÷5   457÷5   1,938÷5

Dividing by 4 Piece-by-Piece

When dividing by 4, the "good" numbers for us are the ones on the Count By 4s list:

4, 8, 12, 16, 20, 24, 28, 32, 36, 40

Each of these numbers with a 0 at the end is also good for us:

40, 80, 120, 160, 200, 240, 280, 320, 360, 400

Let us do a couple of examples, and then you do a few on your own:

For example: $735 \div 4 = (400 + 320 + 15) \div 4$
Now ask: How many 4s go into 400? How many go into 320? How may go into 15?
Answer: 100 + 80 + 3 (remainder 3) = 183 R3

Another example: $823 \div 4 = (400 + 400 + 23) \div 4$
Now ask: How many 4s go into 400? How many go into 23?
Answer: 100 + 100 + 5 (remainder 3) = 205 R3

Now try to divide the following numbers by 4 on your own: remember that the key is to break the numbers into pieces that are easy to divide by 4 from the lists above.

$127 \div 4$ $347 \div 4$ $738 \div 4$

$175 \div 4$ $657 \div 4$ $4{,}938 \div 4$

Dividing by 9 Piece-by-Piece

When dividing by 9, the "good" numbers for us are the ones on the Count By 9s list:

9, 18, 27, 36, 45, 54, 63, 72, 81, 90

Each of these numbers with a 0 at the end is also good for us:

90, 180, 270, 360, 450, 540, 630, 720, 810, 900

Let us do a couple of examples, and then you do a few on your own:

For example: $735 \div 9 = (720 + 15) \div 9$
Now ask: How many 9s go into 720? How many go into 15?
Answer: 80 + 1 (remainder 6) = 81 R6

Another example: $313 = (270 + 43) \div 9$
Now ask: How many 9s go into 270? How many go into 43?
Answer: 30 + 4 (remainder 7) = 34 R7

Now try to divide the following numbers by 9 on your own: remember that the key is to break the numbers into pieces that are easy to divide by 9 from the lists above.

$127 \div 9$ $377 \div 9$ $638 \div 9$

$195 \div 9$ $1,657 \div 9$ $4,938 \div 9$

POWERS and EXPONENTS: WHAT ARE THEY?

base $\longrightarrow 3^4 = 3 \cdot 3 \cdot 3 \cdot 3$ (exponent, power)

$$2 \times 2 = 2^2 = 4$$
$$2 \times 2 \times 2 = 2^3 = 8$$
$$2 \times 2 \times 2 \times 2 = 2^4 = 16$$
$$2 \times 2 \times 2 \times 2 \times 2 = 2^5 = 32$$
$$2 \times 2 \times 2 \times 2 \times 2 \times 2 = 2^6 = 64$$
$$2 \times 2 \times 2 \times 2 \times 2 \times 2 \times 2 = 2^7 = 128$$

Powers are used as shorthand when we multiply a number BY ITSELF. For example, when we multiply 2 by itself five times, instead of writing $2 \times 2 \times 2 \times 2 \times 2$, we can simply write 2^5. This saves us time. In words we say "2 to the power of 5". The number 2 in this case is the BASE, and 5 is the POWER. The power tells us how many times we have to multiply the base by itself to get the answer.

A.   Now try a few on your own. Calculate the following:

Example: $8^2 = 8 \times 8 = 64$

1. $3^2 =$ _____ = _____
2. $5^2 =$ _____ = _____
3. $6^2 =$ _____ = _____
4. $1^2 =$ _____ = _____
5. $10^2 =$ _____ = _____
6. $4^2 =$ _____ = _____

When the power is equal to 2, we can say "to the power of 2", but we can also say "squared". For example, we can describe 7^2 as "7 to the power of 2" and also "7 squared". In both cases it means the same thing: 7×7. So SQUARING a number is really multiplying it by itself.

B.   Calculate the following:

1.   3 squared = _____ = _____
2.   9 squared = _____ = _____
3.   6 to the power of 2 = _____ = _____
4.   0 squared = _____ = _____
5.   5 to the power of 2 = _____ = _____

C.   Calculate the following:

1. 1^2 = _____ = _____
2. 1^3 = _____ = _____
3. 1^5 = _____ = _____
4. 1^{10} = _____ = _____
5. 1^4 = _____ = _____

What do you observe? **The number 1 to ANY power is always _____**

D.   Calculate the following:

1. 0^2 = _____ = _____
2. 0^3 = _____ = _____
3. 0^5 = _____ = _____
4. 0^{10} = _____ = _____
5. 0^4 = _____ = _____

What do you observe? **The number 0 to ANY power is always _____**

E.   Write the following as POWERS. No need to calculate the result

1. $7 \times 7 \times 7$ = _____
2. $10 \times 10 \times 10 \times 10 \times 10$ = _____
3. $6 \times 6 \times 6 \times 6 \times 6 \times 6 \times 6 \times 6 \times 6$ = _____
4. $12 \times 12 \times 12 \times 12$ = _____
5. $3 \times 3 \times 3 \times 3 \times 3 \times 3$ = _____
6. 8 = _____

F.   Calculate the following:

1. 3^1 = _____
2. 8^1 = _____
3. 34^1 = _____
4. 0^1 = _____
5. 500^1 = _____
6. $1,000^1$ = _____

What do you observe? **ANY number to the power of 1 is _____**

G.   Calculate the following POWERS and know them BY HEART:

1. 2^2 = _____   2. 2^3 = _____   3. 2^4 = _____

4. 2^5 = _____   5. 2^6 = _____   6. 2^7 = _____

7. 2^8 = _____   8. 2^9 = _____   9. 2^{10} = _____

H.   Calculate the following POWERS and learn them BY HEART:

1. 3^2 = _____   2. 3^3 = _____   3. 3^4 = _____

4. 3^5 = _____   5. 3^6 = _____

6. 4^2 = _____   7. 4^3 = _____   8. 4^4 = _____

9. 5^2 = _____   10. 5^3 = _____   11. 5^4 = _____

12. 6^2 = _____   13. 6^3 = _____   14. 7^2 = _____

15. 7^3 = _____   16. 8^2 = _____   17. 8^3 = _____

18. 9^2 = _____   19. 9^3 = _____

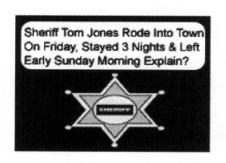

POSITIVES AND NEGATIVES

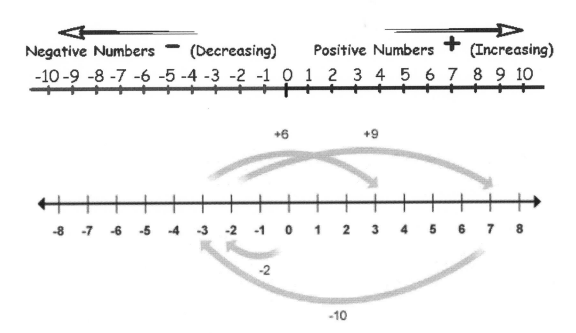

A. Solve the following (visualize a number line):

$7 - 6 =$ $8 - 3 =$ $20 - 4 =$

$6 - 7 =$ $3 - 8 =$ $4 - 20 =$

What is the relationship between $(A - B)$ and $(B - A)$?

B. Solve the following:

$70 - 60 =$ _____ $80 - 30 =$ _____ $90 - 10 =$ _____

$60 - 70 =$ _____ $30 - 80 =$ _____ $10 - 90 =$ _____

$700 - 600 =$ _____ $800 - 300 =$ _____ $900 - 100 =$ _____

$600 - 700 =$ _____ $300 - 800 =$ _____ $100 - 900 =$ _____

$7000 - 6000 =$ _____ $8000 - 3000 =$ _____ $9000 - 1000 =$ _____

$6000 - 7000 =$ _____ $3000 - 8000 =$ _____ $1000 - 9000 =$ _____

MENTAL SUBTRACTION

Subtracting Left to Right using positive and negative numbers

This is a GREAT method because it allows us to do subtraction in our head easily!

Example: Calculate 843 – 389 in your head

Work your way from LEFT TO RIGHT. Start with the hundreds: 800 minus 300 is 500. Remember the 500. Move on to the tens: 40 minus 80 is -40, so from the 500 we take away 40 to get 460. Remember the 460. Lastly do the ones: 3 minus 9 is -6, so the final answer is 460 minus 6, or **454**. There is nothing to write down as we go.

C. Use the method above to solve these **in your head**:

72 – 43 =_____   76 – 35 =_____   91 – 17 =_____

64 – 29 =_____   86 – 29 =_____   89 – 25 =_____

745 – 626 = _____   821 – 375 = _____   911 – 177 =_____

629 – 146 = _____   875 – 321 = _____   467 – 258 =_____

731 – 337 =_____   811 – 308 =_____   944 – 121 =_____

665 – 388 =_____   668 – 129 =_____   829 – 530 =_____

OPTICAL ILLUSIONS

Can you count the black dots?

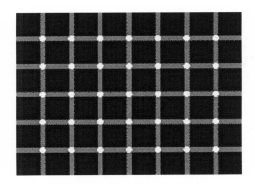

Musician playing the saxophone or a young woman?

Which of the two circles in the center is bigger?

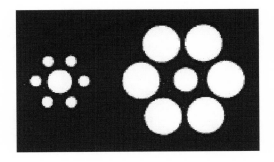

Rabbit or duck?

Young girl or old woman?

A face of an Indian Chief or an Inuit (Eskimo) entering a cave?

How many legs does the elephant have?

AND THE BEST ONE Of THEM ALL....

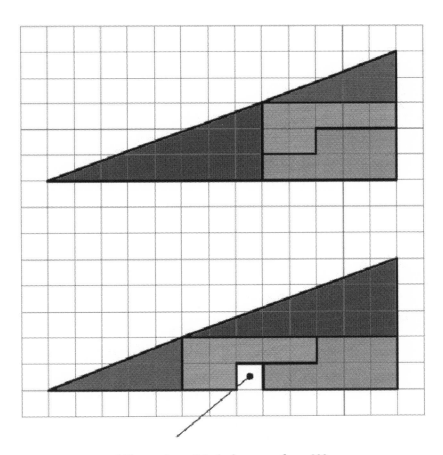

Where does this hole come from???

Inky #1

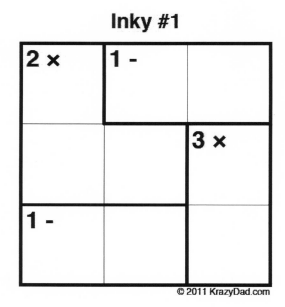

Inky #2

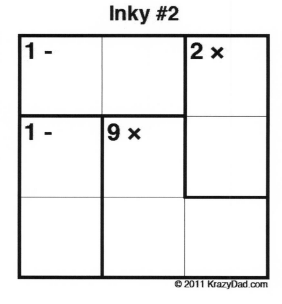

Inky #3

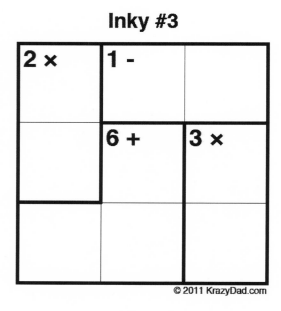

Inky #4

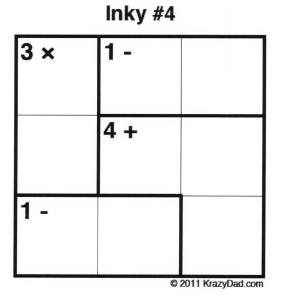

Inky #5

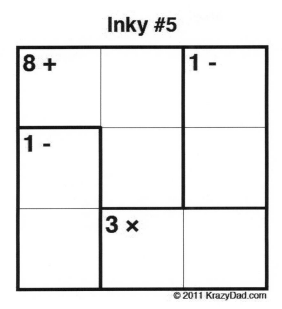

© 2011 KrazyDad.com

Inky #6

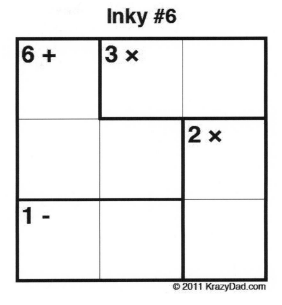

© 2011 KrazyDad.com

Inky #7

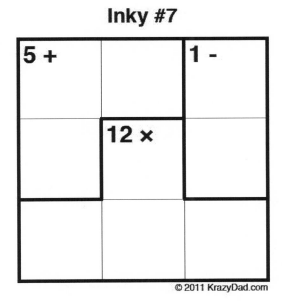

© 2011 KrazyDad.com

Inky #8

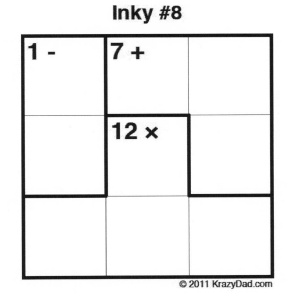

© 2011 KrazyDad.com

Inky #1

2 /	1 -		1 -
	4 ×	2 /	
12 +			4 ×

Inky #2

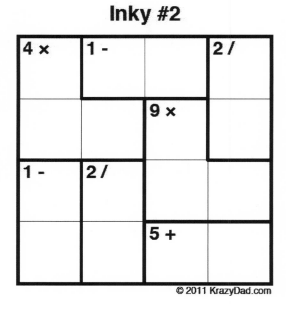

Inky #3

Inky #4

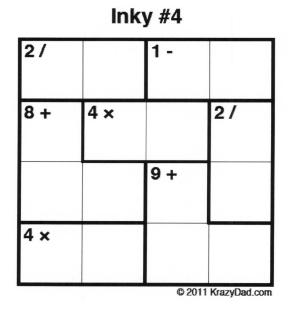

Inky #5

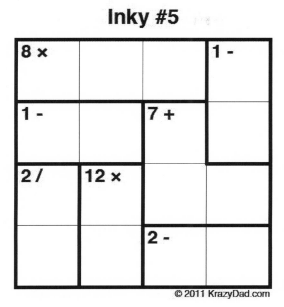

Inky #6

Inky #7

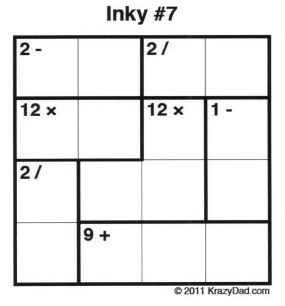

Inky #8

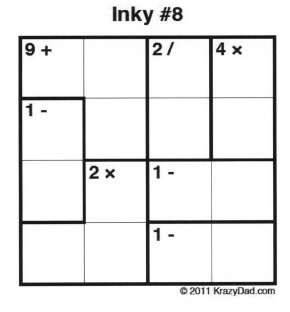

Sudoku #1

2		5			7			6
4			9	6		2		
			8				4	5
9	8			7	4			
5	7		8		2		6	9
			6	3			5	7
7	5			2				
	6			5	1			2
3			4			5		8

Sudoku #2

	6				5	7		2
		4		9	6		1	
8	7	1	3		2			
5				7	1	3		
	3			5			7	
		7	8	2				5
			5		9	6	8	7
	8			2	6		1	
7			6	4			2	

Economy makes men independent.

Sudoku #3

4	7		9		1	6		5
	2		3				8	4
								1
	1	4	7		8		5	
6			2		3			9
	3		6		5	8	1	
8								
5	9				4		2	
7		1	5		2		9	8

Sudoku #4

5				4		6	9	7
8				2			4	
		9	5		3	1		8
		1	4	3			7	
			7		9			
	7			6	5	4		
1		3	2		4	7		
	2		9					4
6	9	4		1				5

Problem of the Week: Making $10.00

Eesha took her friend Jack to her fav**o**rite ice cream place, Dairy Queen, to chill with a Blizzard. They bought two blizza**r**ds for $8.15, and gave a $10.00. When Eesha got her change of $1.85 sh**e** n**o**ticed right away that it has the exa**c**t same digits that are in the amount she paid (1, 8 and 5).

Jack then said "I bet you there are other amounts of money that if you pay them with a $10.**00** bill, what you pay and what you get back will have the exact same digits".

1. Is Ja**ck** right, or is the combination $8.15 and $1.85 the only one?
2. If Jack is r**i**ght, how many combinations ar**e** there that work like thi**s**?
3. What flavor of Blizzard did they order?

In **BRIDGES PROBLEMS** you have to find a walk that crosses each and every bridge once and only once.

You may start and finish at any point

BRIDGES Puzzle 1

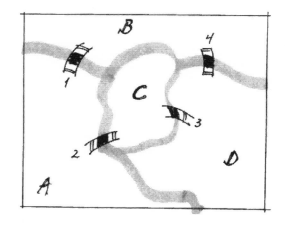

BRIDGES Puzzle 2

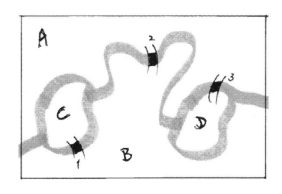

BRIDGES Puzzle 3

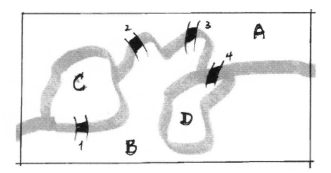

BRIDGES Puzzle 4

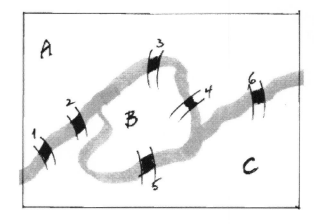

BRIDGES of Konigsberg (Puzzle 5)

BRIDGES Puzzle 6

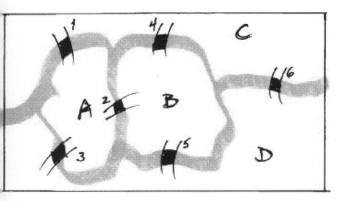

BRIDGES Puzzle 7

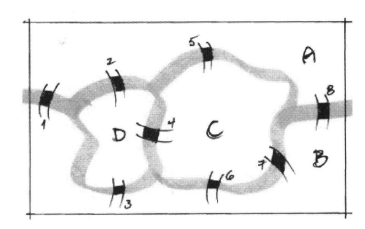

BRIDGES Puzzle 8

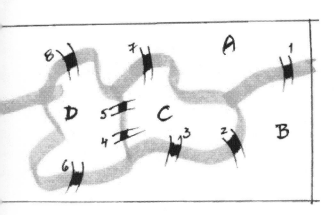

BRIDGES Puzzle 9

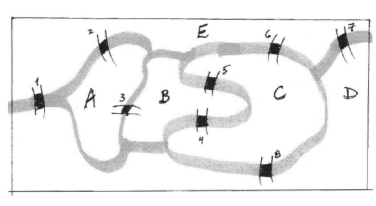

BRIDGES Puzzle 10

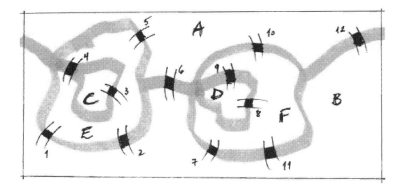

BRIDGES Puzzle 11

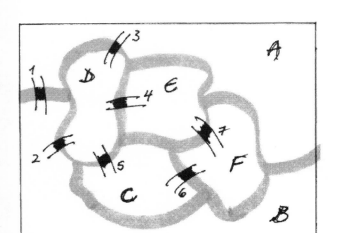

BRIDGES Puzzle 12

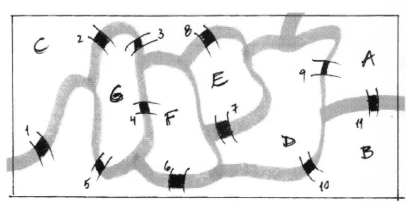

BRIDGES Puzzle 13

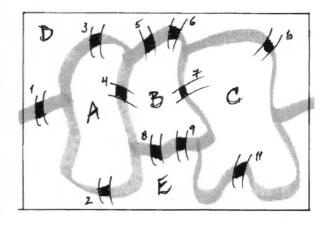

BRIDGES Puzzle 14

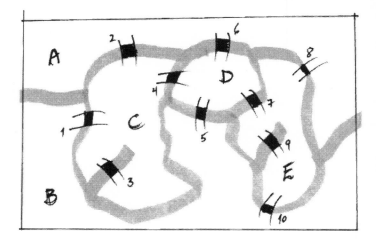

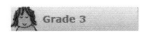

IXL Grade 3 Activities appropriate for the 3B LEVEL

Addition
C.8 Addition patterns over increasing place values
C.9 Add two numbers with four or more digits
C.10 Addition input/output tables - four or more digits
C.11 Add two numbers with four or more digits - word problems
C.12 Complete the addition sentence - four or more digits
C.13 Balance equations - four or more digits
C.14 Add three or more numbers with four or more digits
C.15 Add three or more numbers with four or more digits - word problems
C.16 Addition: fill in the missing digits

Subtraction
D.6 Subtraction patterns over increasing place values
D.7 Subtract numbers with four or more digits
D.8 Subtraction input/output tables - four or more digits
D.9 Subtraction: fill in the missing digits

Multiplication skill builders
F.12 Multiply by 11
F.13 Multiply by 12

Multiplication fluency
G.11 Multiplication tables up to 12x12
G.12 Multiplication facts up to 12x12: find the missing factor

Multiplication
H.7 Multiply one-digit numbers by two-digit numbers
H.8 Multiply one-digit numbers by two-digit numbers: word problems
H.9 Multiply one-digit numbers by three-digit numbers
H.10 Multiply one-digit numbers by three-digit numbers: word problems
H.11 Multiply three or more numbers
H.12 Multiply three or more numbers: word problems
H.13 Box multiplication
H.14 Lattice multiplication

Division skill builders
J.6 Divide by 6
J.7 Divide by 7
J.8 Divide by 8
J.9 Divide by 9
J.11 Divide by 11
J.12 Divide by 12
Division fluency

K.3 Division facts for 6, 7, 8, and 9
K.4 Division facts for 6, 7, 8, and 9: true or false?
K.5 Division facts up to 10x10
K.6 Division facts up to 10x10: true or false?
K.7 Division facts up to 10x10: sorting
K.8 Division facts up to 10x10: find the missing number
K.9 Division sentences up to 10x10: true or false?
K.10 Division facts to 12x12

Division
L.1 Divide numbers ending in zeroes
L.2 Division patterns over increasing place values
L.3 Division input/output tables
L.4 Division word problems
L.5 Divide larger numbers
L.6 Divide larger numbers: word problems
L.7 Divisibility rules for 2, 5 and 10

Mixed operations
M.4 Multiplication and division facts up to 10x10: true or false?
M.5 Multiplication and division facts up to 12x12: true or false?
M.6 Multiplication and division sentences up to 12x12: true or false?

Properties
N.1 Addition, subtraction, multiplication and division terms
N.2 Understanding parentheses
N.3 Properties of addition
N.4 Solve using properties of addition
N.5 Properties of multiplication
N.6 Solve using properties of multiplication
N.7 Distributive property: find the missing factor
N.8 Multiply using the distributive property
N.9 Relate addition and multiplication
N.10 Relate multiplication and division

Estimation and rounding
P.1 Rounding
P.2 Round money amounts
P.3 Rounding puzzles
P.4 Solve inequalities using estimation
P.5 Estimate sums
P.6 Estimate differences
P.7 Estimate products
P.8 Estimate quotients

Logical reasoning

Q.1 Guess the number
Q.2 Largest/smallest number possible
Q.3 Find the order
Q.4 Age puzzles
Q.5 Find two numbers based on sum and difference
Q.6 Find two numbers based on sum, difference, product and quotient

Compare and order fractions
AA.1 Graph and compare fractions with like numerators on number lines
AA.2 Graph and compare fractions with like denominators on number lines
AA.3 Graph and compare fractions on number lines
AA.4 Compare fractions with like denominators
AA.5 Compare fractions
AA.6 Order fractions with like denominators
AA.7 Order fractions

IXL GRADE 4 Activities appropriate for the 3B Level

Number sense
A.1 Place values
A.2 Convert between place values
A.3 Word names for numbers
A.4 Roman numerals
A.6 Rounding
A.7 Even or odd: arithmetic rules
A.8 Inequalities with number lines
A.9 Put numbers up to four digits in order
A.10 Compare numbers up to five digits

Addition
B.1 Add numbers up to five digits
B.2 Add numbers up to five digits: word problems
B.3 Addition: fill in the missing digits
B.4 Properties of addition
B.5 Add three or more numbers up to five digits each
B.6 Addition patterns over increasing place values
B.7 Choose numbers with a particular sum
B.8 Estimate sums
B.9 Estimate sums: word problems
Subtraction
C.1 Subtract numbers up to five digits
C.2 Subtract numbers up to five digits: word problems
C.3 Subtraction: fill in the missing digits
C.4 Subtraction patterns over increasing place values
C.5 Choose numbers with a particular difference

F.8 Mentally add and subtract numbers ending in zeroes
F.9 Inequalities involving addition, subtraction, multiplication and division

Logical reasoning
I.1 Find two numbers based on sum and difference
I.2 Find two numbers based on sum, difference, product and quotient
I.3 Find the order

Patterns and sequences
J.1 Find the next shape in a repeating pattern
J.2 Complete a repeating pattern
J.3 Make a repeating pattern
J.4 Find the next row in a growing pattern of shapes
J.5 Complete an increasing number pattern
J.6 Complete a geometric number pattern
J.7 Number patterns: word problems
J.8 Number patterns: mixed review

Data and graphs
L.1 Read a table
L.2 Interpret line graphs
L.3 Create line graphs
L.4 Interpret bar graphs
L.5 Create bar graphs
L.6 Interpret line plots
L.7 Create line plots
L.8 Frequency charts
L.9 Stem-and-leaf plots
L.10 Circle graphs
L.11 Choose the best type of graph

Money
M.1 Compare money amounts
M.2 Round money amounts
M.3 Add and subtract money amounts
M.4 Making change
M.5 Price lists

Geometry
P.1 Identify two-dimensional and three-dimensional figures
P.2 Count and compare sides, edges, faces and vertices
P.3 Which two-dimensional figure is being described?
P.4 Which three-dimensional figure is being described?
P.5 Nets of three-dimensional figures
P.6 Is it a polygon?
P.7 Number of sides in polygons
P.8 Lines, line segments and rays
P.9 Parallel, perpendicular and intersecting lines

P.10Acute, right, obtuse and straight angles
P.11Types of triangles
P.12Similar and congruent
P.13Identify lines of symmetry

Geometric measurement

Q.1Perimeter
Q.2Find the area of figures made of unit squares
Q.3Create figures with a given area
Q.4Find the area or missing side length of a rectangle
Q.5Area and perimeter: word problems

Understand Fractions

R.1Understand fractions: fraction bars
R.2Understand fractions: area models
R.3Match fractions to models
R.4Show fractions: fraction bars
R.5Show fractions: area models
R.6Understanding fractions: word problems

Compare and order fractions

T.1Compare fractions with like numerators or denominators using models
T.2Compare fractions with like numerators or denominators
T.3Compare fractions using models
T.4Compare fractions
T.5Graph and compare fractions on number lines
T.6Benchmark fractions
T.7Compare fractions using benchmarks
T.8Compare fractions in recipes
T.9Order fractions with like numerators or denominators
T.10Order fractions
T.11Find smaller or larger fractions

3B Final Assessment

1. Fill in the blanks:

a. 1,370 is _____ less than 6,000

b. 12,370 is 1,200 more than _____

c. When 356 is divided by 5, the quotient is _____, and the remainder is _____

d. Write the number eleven thousand, three hundred and forty: _____

e. The sum of 12,370 and 1,900 is _____

f. When 356 is divided by 5, the quotient is _____, and the remainder is _____

g. The difference between 2,000 and 890 is _____

h. The product of 12 and 50 is _____

i. My favourite math teacher is _____

2. Waseem gave his brother Kareem $24.50 for his birthday, and then gave him another $37.85 for being a nice brother. How much money did Waseem give Kareem in total?

3. An iPad and 5 identical apples weigh 1,610 grams. The iPad alone weighs 660 grams. What is the weight of a single apple?

4. In Mr. Merrick's farm, there are 7 times as many llamas as donkeys, and 53 less ostriches than llamas. How many ostriches are there on the farm, if we know that there are 13 donkeys?

5. Dr. Vince loves math and wrestling. He gave Chris Jericho $3,450. Chris bought a wrestling gown for $1,870, gave his pet lizard Vlad $350, and donated the rest to children who wrestle in Africa. How much did Chris donate?

6. Solve the following multiplication and division questions:

a. $16 \times 5 =$ _____

b. $129 \div 5 =$ _____

c. $7 \times 22 =$ _____

d. $404 \div 7 =$ _____

e. $9 \times 9 =$ _____

f. $388 \div 6 =$ _____

7. Shrek has 340 lemons. He threw away 26 that were rotten, and gave each of his friends 11 lemons. At the end he had less than 11 lemons left, so he gave them to Fiona.

a. How many friends does he have?

b. How many lemons did he give to Fiona?

8. Solve the following mentally:

a. $1,317 + 458 =$ _____

b. $9,029 - 5,948 =$ _____

c. $7,952 + 3,415 =$ _____

d. $8,304 - 2,185 =$ _____

9. Musa has $46, which his half of what his brother Yahya has. Their dad, Nabil, has $75 more than what both boys have together. Nabil used his money to buy a Hookah for $175. How much money did Nabil have left?

10. + + = 48

   × = 80

   + − = ?

11. Solve the following multiplication and division questions:

a. $316 \times 6 = $ _____

b. $1{,}029 \div 5 = $ _____

c. $7 \times 415 = $ _____

d. $4{,}304 \div 7 = $ _____

e. $9 \times 927 = $ _____

f. $3{,}188 \div 6 = $ _____

12. No need to explain what you have to do here:

🍎 + 🍎 + 🍎 = 120

🍎 + 🍌 + 🍌 = 100

🍌 + 🍎 + 🍎 = 105

🍌 + 🍎 = ?

COMPETITION CORNER

Welcome to competition corner. In this section we will explore some of the best math competitions around. The purpose of partaking in math contests is to have fun, appreciate mathematics, and get stronger by going over past competition forms. At Bright Minds, two of our favourite contests for our elementary school students are:

i. Calgary Elementary School Math Contest (CESMC)

ii. MathLeague

Remember that as you reach the end of a form the problems increase in difficulty and are meant to be challenging. It is perfectly OK to struggle, and not to be able to solve them all. We hope you enjoy them as much as all of us at Renert School.

For Parents:

For added resources and training, please visit:

1. CESMC: http://blogs.mtroyal.ca/cesmc/sample-test/

2. MathLeague: https://www.mathleague.com/index.php/annualcontestinformation/samplecontests

You will find past contest forms with complete solutions on both sites. We thank Mount Royal University (Calgary, Canada) and The Math League (United States) for providing these materials to math enthusiasts in order to spread mathematical literacy. Any student who is working on the Bright Minds level-3 booklets should be able to tackle the CESMC Level I, as well as MathLeague Grade-4 forms. Competition training is one of the most powerful ways to get a child to become a stronger problem solver.

ENJOY and GOOD LUCK!!!

Calgary Elementary School Mathematics Contest (2012)
LEVEL-1 SAMPLE CONTEST

PART A: Circle the correct answer. Each correct answer is worth **5 points.**

1. $(2 + 3 + 4 + 5 + 6) - (5 + 4 + 3 + 2) =$

   (a) 6   (b) 5   (c) 4   (d) 3

2. A piece of string is 4m long. It is cut into pieces that are 20 cm long. How many pieces are there?

   (a) 2   (b) 5   (c) 16   (d) 20

3. If the time is now 1:45PM and my clock stopped running 3 and a quarter hours ago, at what time did my clock stop?

   (a) 10:30AM   (b) 10:45AM   (c) 4:45PM   (d) 5:00PM

4. Find the missing number: $6 + 12 + 18 + 24 + 30 = ? \times (1 + 2 + 3 + 4 + 5)$.

   (a) 3   (b) 6   (c) 9   (d) 12

5. If you buy a pack of a dozen apples you pay $5.50. A single apple costs 50 cents. How much do you save if you buy a pack of a dozen apples?

   (a) $0.50   (b) $0.60   (c) $5.00   (d) $6.00

6. Peter has 2 quarters, 1 dime, 1 nickel and 2 pennies. How much money does Peter have?

   (a) 57 cents   (b) 62 cents   (c) 65 cents   (d) 67 cents

7. Ann reads all pages in a book, starting from page 31 and finishing on page 50. How many pages did she read?

   (a) 19   (b) 20   (c) 31   (d) 50

8. The product of 2 whole numbers is 7. What is their sum?

   (a) 7   (b) 8   (c) 9   (d) 14

9. What is one half of one fifth of 50?

   (a) 2   (b) 4   (c) 5   (d) 6

10. A whole number is multiplied by 14. The product could <u>never</u> be

   (a) 0   (b) 42   (c) 80   (d) 84

11. A meal consists of a main dish, a drink, and a dessert. There are 4 different main dishes, 3 different drinks and 5 different desserts. How many different meals are there?

    (a) 12   (b) 17   (c) 19   (d) 60

12. 10 apples weigh the same as 14 pears. 15 apples will weigh the same as how many pears?

    (a) 19   (b) 21   (c) 24   (d) 29

13. Find the missing number: $5 \times (6 \times 7) = 5 \times 6 + ?$

    (a) 30   (b) 37   (c) 180   (d) 210

14. The perimeter of a square is 20. What is the area of the square?

    (a) 25   (b) 125   (c) 250   (d) 400

15. Which equation is false?

    (a) $\frac{18}{10} = 1.8$ (b) $\frac{1}{10} + \frac{1}{100} = 0.11$ (c) $\frac{1}{1000} = 0.01$ (d) $1 + \frac{13}{10} = 2.3$

16. If the area of the shaded region of the square is 36, then the area of the square is

    (a) 48

    (b) 72

    (c) 96

    (d) 120

    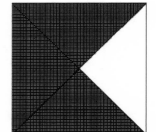

17. A jar completely filled with water weighs 5000 grams. The same jar, half-filled with water weighs 3250 grams. How much does the empty jar weigh?

    (a) 1500 g   (b) 1625 g   (c) 1750 g   (d) 2500 g

18. How many more triangles than squares are shown in the picture?

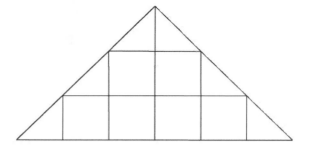

(a) 6

(b) 7

(c) 8

(d) 9

19. In the figure below, $ACDH$ and $BCEF$ are rectangles. If $AC = 10$cm and $CE = 15$cm, what is the perimeter of the figure $ACEFGHA$?

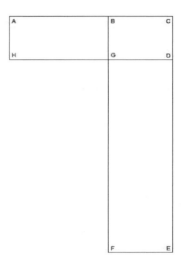

(a) 25cm

(b) 35cm

(c) 40cm

(d) 50cm

20. A store sells envelopes in packages of 5 and 7 envelopes each. It is impossible to buy exactly

(a) 17 envelopes   (b) 23 envelopes   (c) 26 envelopes   (d) 32 envelopes

(a) 17 envelopes

(b) 23 envelopes

(c) 26 envelopes

(d) 32 envelopes

Sample 4th Grade Contest

Spring, 2019

Instructions

4

	2018-2019 4TH GRADE CONTEST	Answers
1.	Which of the following sums and products is an odd number? A) 2018×2019 B) 2019×2020 C) $2018 + 2019$ D) $2019 + 2021$	1.
2.	If Zach multiplied the whole number on his shirt by itself, which of the following could be his result? A) 24 B) 25 C) 26 D) 27	2.
3.	What is the product of 49 ones? A) 1 B) 7 C) 49 D) 50	3.
4.	4 dozen socks = _?_ pairs of socks A) 2 B) 24 C) 48 D) 96	4.
5.	If the number of months in a year is divided by the number of days in a week, what is the remainder? A) 0 B) 2 C) 5 D) 7	5.
6.	Henry the Hamster first danced on November 1, 2018. By April 1, 2019, for how many months had he been dancing? A) 5 B) 6 C) 7 D) 8	6.
7.	$20 - 18 + 20 - 18 + 20 - 18 = ?$ A) 2 B) 4 C) 6 D) 8	7.
8.	What is the ones digit in the product $12 \times 13 \times 14$? A) 2 B) 4 C) 6 D) 8	8.
9.	Which of the following is greatest? A) $1 \times 2 \times 12$ B) $2 \times 3 \times 4$ C) $4 \times 2 \times 2$ D) $2 \times 4 \times 4$	9.
10.	Sandra uses two entire erasers for every 15 questions she answers. If erasers come in packs of 12, at least how many packs does she need for her 100-question test? A) 2 B) 3 C) 4 D) 5	10.
11.	The greatest whole-number multiple of 7 that is less than 100 is A) 91 B) 93 C) 97 D) 98	11.
12.	The digit _?_ appears only one time in the sum of 654 and 456. A) 0 B) 1 C) 2 D) 3	12.

2018-2019 4TH GRADE CONTEST   **Answers**

13. Ella wears a sweater of a different color each day of the week—red for | 13.
    Sundays, blue for Mondays, etc. Each of her many sweaters is one of 7
    different colors. She donates each sweater to charity after wearing it 4
    times! The least number of sweaters Ella wears during December is

    A) 7   B) 8   C) 10   D) 12

14. How many whole numbers greater than 10 and less than 200 can be | 14.
    written using only even digits?

    A) 16   B) 20   C) 25   D) 50

15. Noah has a soccer game every day and scores two goals in every | 15.
    game. How many weeks will it take him to score 56 goals?

    A) 3   B) 4   C) 5   D) 18

16. Chris ran each lap of his 10-lap race in 90 | 16.
    seconds. After running for 6 minutes, how
    many laps did Chris have *left* to run?

    A) 3   B) 4   C) 5   D) 6

17. How many pairs of unequal whole numbers | 17.
    greater than 40 and less than 60 sum to 100?

    A) 9   B) 10   C) 18   D) 20

18. $2 \times 4 \times 5 \times 25 = ?$ | 18.

    A) 6×125 B) 6×150 C) 8×150 D) 10×100

19. The average of 3 numbers is a whole number. If one number is 2, | 19.
    and the other 2 numbers are equal, the other numbers could each be

    A) 3   B) 4   C) 5   D) 6

20. $2000 - 200¢ + \$20 - 2¢ =$ | 20.

    A) $1999.98   B) $2017.80   C) $2017.98   D) $2020.20

21. Joey has only large and small boxes. In each | 21.
    large box there are exactly four small boxes. If
    Joey has 20 boxes total, the lowest possible
    number of small boxes that Joey has is

    A) 4   B) 5   C) 15   D) 16

22. How many whole numbers between 100 and 200 are divisible by | 22.
    both 4 and 6?

    A) 6   B) 7   C) 8   D) 10

23. Jake bought cheese slices to put on his daily sandwich. If he puts 6 cheese slices on each sandwich, then one day he will have 2 cheese slices left over. If he puts 5 cheese slices on each sandwich, then one day he will have 3 cheese slices left over. He could have started with __?__ cheese slices.

    A) 13　　　　B) 14　　　　C) 26　　　　D) 38

    23.

24. In Olive's kingdom, castles have 8 beds and homes have 2 beds. If there are 48 beds and 3 castles, how many homes are there?

    A) 12　　B) 16　　C) 24　　D) 48

    24.

25. How many whole numbers greater than 100 and less than 1000 have all three digits different from one another?

    A) 648　　B) 720　　C) 729　　D) 900

    25.

26. Of the following intervals, which includes the most prime numbers?

    A) 20 and 30　　B) 30 and 40　　C) 40 and 50　　D) 50 and 60

    26.

27. Simona has only dimes and quarters, which total exactly one dollar. If she has at least one dime and at least one quarter, how many coins **must** she have all together?

    A) 4　　　　B) 7　　　　C) 9　　　　D) 10

    27.

28. Briana can solve 6 puzzle cubes in 4 minutes, and Avima can solve 5 puzzle cubes in 6 minutes. At these rates, Briana can solve one cube __?__ seconds more quickly than Avima can.

    A) 24　　B) 27　　C) 30　　D) 32

    28.

29. __?__ is the product of exactly 2 prime numbers.

    A) 2018　　B) 2020　　C) 3018　　D) 3020

    29.

30. At most how many 1-by-3 rectangles that do not overlap can fit in a 5-by-7 rectangle?

    A) 9　　　　B) 10　　　　C) 11　　　　D) 12

    30.

Marking Key - Guide to Parents and Markers

The reason we include a marking key at the end of each booklet is so students can tell in real time whether they understand the material and are getting the correct answers. Solving math problems without knowing if you are doing it correctly is time-wasteful, and even pointless. This is where you, the parent, can greatly help both your child, as well as the teacher.

How to do it right? Please follow these guidelines closely:

- Grab your favourite yellow highlighter.

- Place a checkmark ✓ with a pen beside any question the child gets correct.

- HIGHLIGHT with a yellow highlighter the question number of any question the child got wrong. If the question is unnumbered, you can highlight the wrong answer itself.

- Ask the child to go over their mistakes, and try to correct, to the best of their ability. If it is a careless error, the child should be able to find and correct it. If it is an error that stems from lack of understanding of how to solve the question, this is fine. We will explain the concept again to the child in class and guide him to the solution.

- We do not expect you to teach your child any of the mathematical concepts at home. This is our job, but it speeds us tremendously when the marking was done at home, so we can see very quickly where the child went wrong.

- Do NOT spoon feed solutions to your child or guide them too heavily. As instructors we always assume that a correct answer is one that the child worked out, and that if asked how they got it, they should be able to explain. Making many mistakes is part of the learning process and **there is nothing wrong with it**. As a parent you have to get very comfortable with your child making mistakes. You will speed your child up, however, by highlighting these mistakes and asking the child if they can correct them unassisted.

- Feel free to communicate with the instructor by jotting comments in the booklet and asking your child to show them to the instructor. For instance, you may write "really struggles with long division, but understands very well short division..." etc. Again, it helps our instructors a great deal in knowing what to zoom in on.

- Marking key is to use, not abuse. If the child starts copying answers wholesale and presents them as their own, explain to them how unproductive it is, and that they should not do it.

You can access the **3B digital marking key** at: https://bit.ly/3ahwHCP

HOMEWORK TRACKING

HOMEWORK TRACKING

Made in the USA
Middletown, DE
22 December 2021